CRYSTAL STEMWARE

IDENTIFICATION GUIDE

from

REPLACEMENTS, LTD.

China, Crystal & Flatware · Discontinued & Active

Bob Page
&
Dale
Frederiksen

COLLECTOR BOOKS

A Division of Schroeder Publishing Co., Inc.

A special thanks is given to all of the individuals involved, no matter how small or great their part, in the compiling of the information in this guide. The staffs of the crystal, research, and imaging services departments at Replacements, Ltd. have been invaluable in the completion of this guide, with many hours spent on the identifying, verifying, and photographing of stemware patterns.

Searching For A Publisher?

We are always looking for knowledgeable people considered to be experts within their fields. If you feel that there is a real need for a book on your collectible subject and have a large comprehensive collection, contact Collector Books.

Cover design by Beth Summers

Additional copies of this book may be ordered from:

Collector Books
P.O. Box 3009
Paducah, Kentucky 42002-3009

@$18.95. Add $2.00 for postage and handling.

⬾ _Contents_ ⬾

⊗ *Introduction* ⊗

With more than 4,000 patterns illustrated, this guide is by far the most extensive ever published. We are certain that it will be your #1 source in identifying the crystal patterns that come your way. While not trying to be a comprehensive pattern guide on any one manufacturer, it represents a vast majority of the most collectible and requested stemware patterns of yesterday and today.

This guide is a compilation of a great deal of our resource material covering the many glass manufacturers and importers that are requested today. It includes images from our inventory, as well as representations of patterns based on manufacturer literature, photographs, etc.

Note that Depression glass patterns are not shown in this guide as many reference books are available on these wares.

⊗ *How to Use This Guide* ⊗

We have tried to make researching patterns as easy as possible for you. The layout of the book is alphabetical by manufacturer; since most of the companies represented have only a small number of patterns, your research should be both efficient and successful.

On three of the larger manufacturers, Cambridge, Fostoria, and Heisey, we have included additional information at the beginning of these sections showing the stem or line shapes and the pages on which they appear. With these companies, the patterns are alphabetized and numbered by stem or line number.

For many of the other significantly large companies, we have tried to arrange the patterns in order according to the shape of the stem or bowl. In looking at the various patterns in these pages, the flow will make it much easier to research than if we had simply left these in alphabetical order.

You will notice that some patterns shown throughout the guide are labeled without a conventional name, but instead have a combination of letters and numbers. For example, "7926" by Steuben indicates the style or name of the pattern. Another example would be "896-1" by Bryce. This shows the factory assigned stem number or line, 896, with an unknown design. "ATR 1" by Alsterfors, shown on page 1, is an example of our Replacements, Ltd. manufacturer code followed by our assigned number, since we do not currently know the stem or line number given by the manufacturer.

Some patterns appearing in the guide will be identical from one company to another. Manufacturers such as Spiegelau, Nachtmann, and Schott-Zweisel, major European glassmakers, create many of the wares that are sold by other companies such as Gorham, Mikasa, and Oneida. Sometimes the only difference in a pattern will be the paper label, or if you are indeed fortunate, the manufacturer mark on the base.

We have also supplied you a list of most of the manufacturers that would mark their products on page 369. In most instances, the maker would acid etch their name on the foot of the stemware. In some cases, the name or mark would be engraved in the foot. When the glassware is marked, most often the name of the company is written out. We have also provided other examples of how some companies marked their product. A "•" indicates those companies whose merchandise is almost entirely marked. Care should be taken in purchasing patterns from these companies when the pieces are not marked. Second quality pieces often are unmarked. In the case of Lenox, there is a seconds mark which is a broken circle through the name or around the L.

The final pages in this crystal guide are what we call our Unknown Manufacturers. This section is divided into four smaller units. The first is patterns that have neither a cut nor an etched decoration. The second section contains patterns that are etched or have an encrusted decoration. The third contains cut decorations, and the last section contains pressed patterns. We would appreciate any information that you might have on these unknown patterns.

Drake
Afors

ATR 1
Alsterfors

Jostin
Alsterfors

Lappland
Alsterfors

Aristocrat
American Cut

Barbara
American Cut

Eleanor
American Cut

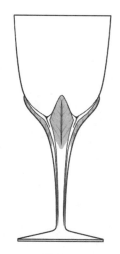

Erica
American Cut
Gray Cut Leaves

Gold Rose
American Cut

Golden Suszy
American Cut

Janice
American Cut

Juliette
American Cut

Leanore
American Cut

Leaves
American Cut

Lima
American Cut

American Cut, American Hostess, American Manor, American Stemware

Princess Irene
American Cut

Roberto
American Cut

Statesmen
American Cut

Tulip
American Cut

Vega
American Cut

Blue Lace
American Hostess

Evangeline
American Hostess

Manor Rose
American Hostess

Spring Glory
American Hostess
Pink or Clear

Ebony
American Manor
Black

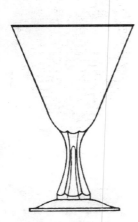

Wedding Day
American Manor
Platinum Trim

Biltmore
American Stemware

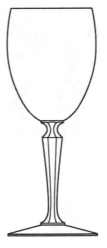

Carmel
American Stemware

Carmel
American Stemware
Gold or Platinum Trim

Carmel
American Stemware
Blue or Pink

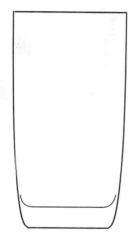

Kenilworth
American Stemware
Clear or with Gold or Plat.

Penthouse Slate
American Stemware
Gray Stem

Princeton
American Stemware

Princeton
American Stemware
Gold or Platinum Trim

Princeton
American Stemware
Frosted Stem

Princeton
American Stemware
Blue or Pink

Sanibel
American Stemware

Westport
American Stemware
Optic

AHC 1
Anchor Hocking

AHC 2
Anchor Hocking

AHC 3
Anchor Hocking

AHC 4
Anchor Hocking

AHC 5
Anchor Hocking

Boopie
Anchor Hocking

Bubble Foot
Anchor Hocking

3

Burple
Anchor Hocking

Laurel
Anchor Hocking

Legend
Anchor Hocking

Medici
Annahuette

Duncan
Arcadia Export-Import

Orlean
Arcadia Export-Import

Celeste
Astral

Christina
Astral

Fantasia Ice
Astral
Gray Cutting

Mira
Astral

Peerage
Astral

Questa
Astral

Starry
Astral

Venus
Astral

Willow
Astral

ATL 1
Atlantis

Algarve
Atlantis

Athena
Atlantis

Azores
Atlantis

Caldas
Atlantis

Cascais
Atlantis

Castelo
Atlantis

Cathay
Atlantis

Celebration
Atlantis

Chalice
Atlantis

Chartres
Atlantis

Coimbra
Atlantis

Column
Atlantis

Diamante
Atlantis

Diana
Atlantis

Elvas
Atlantis

Estoril
Atlantis

Estrella
Atlantis

Evora
Atlantis

Fantasy
Atlantis

Faro
Atlantis

Fatima
Atlantis

Flight
Atlantis

Foliage
Atlantis

Fount
Atlantis

Isabel
Atlantis

Lisbon
Atlantis

Lotus
Atlantis

Lyric
Atlantis

Magellan
Atlantis

Montalegre
Atlantis

Moselle
Atlantis

Nazare
Atlantis

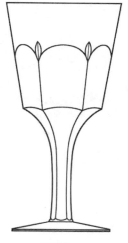

Obidos
Atlantis

Oporto
Atlantis

Palacio
Atlantis

Palmela
Atlantis

Paris
Atlantis

Pillar
Atlantis

Pombal
Atlantis

Sacavem
Atlantis

Santarem
Atlantis

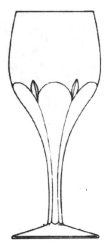

Sara
Atlantis

Setubal
Atlantis

Silves
Atlantis

Sintra
Atlantis

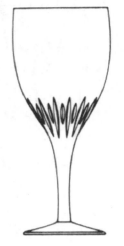

Sonnet
Atlantis
Plain or with Gold Trim

Stripes
Atlantis

Sundial
Atlantis

Tintern
Atlantis

Zephyr
Atlantis

Bridal
Avitra

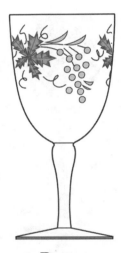

Duncan
Avitra

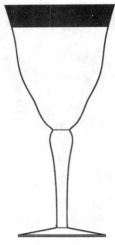

Golden
Avitra

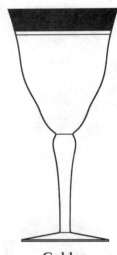

Golden
Avitra
With a hair line

Cape Cod
Avon
Ruby

Emerald Accent
Avon
Green Stem

Hummingbird
Avon
Frosted Stem

Napoleon
Baccarat
Gold "N"

Bacchus
Baccarat
Wine Tasting Glass

Tastevin
Baccarat
aka "Pommard"

Pavillon
Baccarat
aka "Chamberti"

Brummel
Baccarat

Big Ben
Baccarat
aka "Margaux"

Perfection
Baccarat

Montaigne
Baccarat
Non-Optic

Montaigne Optic
Baccarat
Plain or with Gold Trim

Francois Villon
Baccarat

Chateau Lascombes
Baccarat
aka "Antibes"

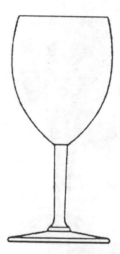

Haut Brion
Baccarat

Chambolle
Baccarat

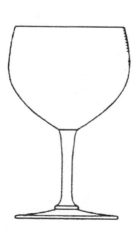

Volnay
Baccarat

Comtesse de Paris
Baccarat

Regence
Baccarat
Gold Trim

Livourne
Baccarat

Brantome
Baccarat

Riberac
Baccarat

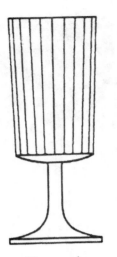

Harmonie
Baccarat

Dom Perignon
Baccarat

St. Remy
Baccarat

Short Tulip
Baccarat
Wine Tasting Glass

Capri
Baccarat
Plain or with Gold Trim

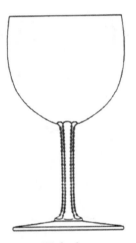

Voltaire
Baccarat

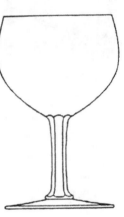

Rabelais
Baccarat

Coppelia
Baccarat

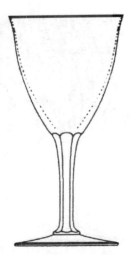

Directoire
Baccarat
Gold Trim

Opera
Baccarat

Avignon
Baccarat

Manon
Baccarat
aka "Mahora," Gold Trim

Normandie
Baccarat

Monte Carlo
Baccarat

Naples
Baccarat

Vienne
Baccarat
Plain or with Gold Trim

Embassy
Baccarat

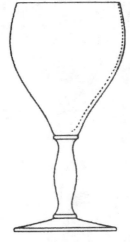

Vincennes
Baccarat

Longchamps
Baccarat

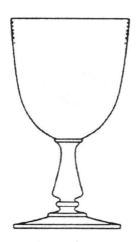

Angouleme
Baccarat

Jose
Baccarat

Gascogne
Baccarat
Smooth Stem

Gascogne
Baccarat
Cut Stem

Provence
Baccarat

Annie
Baccarat
Gold Trim

Vega
Baccarat

Orsay
Baccarat

Oxygéne
Baccarat

Baccarat

Brabant
Baccarat

Sevigne
Baccarat
Etched

Recamier
Baccarat
Etched, Gold Trim & Design

Madame Butterfly
Baccarat
aka "Jersey Lily"

Lafayette
Baccarat

Leillah
Baccarat
Etched

Jasmina
Baccarat
Etched, Gold Trim

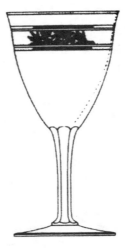

Colorado
Baccarat
Gold Encrusted

Parme
Baccarat

Base Design

Prestige
Baccarat
Gold Encrusted

Rohan
Baccarat
Etched

Marennes
Baccarat

Michelangelo
Baccarat

Orleans
Baccarat

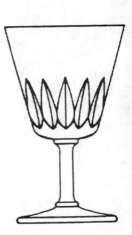

Cote d'Azur
Baccarat

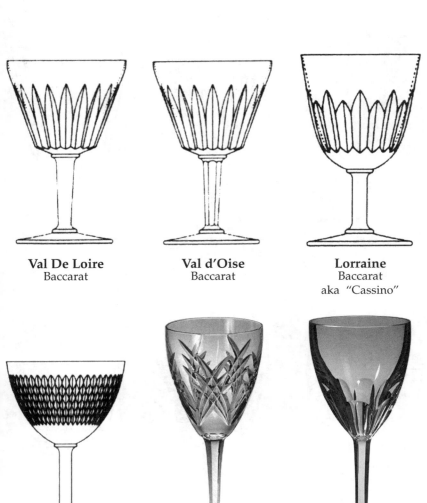

Val De Loire
Baccarat

Val d'Oise
Baccarat

Lorraine
Baccarat
aka "Cassino"

Nancy
Baccarat

Paris
Baccarat

Magenta
Baccarat

Auvergne
Baccarat
aka "Perigord"

Genova
Baccarat

Compiegne
Baccarat

Malmaison
Baccarat

Zurich
Baccarat

Bellinzona
Baccarat

Burgos
Baccarat

Epron
Baccarat

Lagny
Baccarat

Baccarat

Bogota
Baccarat

Condé
Baccarat

Elbeuf
Baccarat

Auteuil
Baccarat

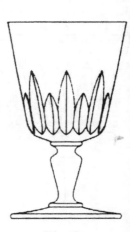

Biarritz
Baccarat

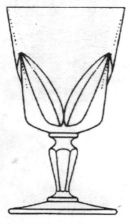

Chartres
Baccarat

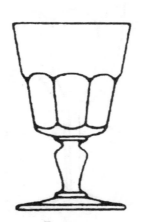

Bretagne
Baccarat
aka "Missouri"

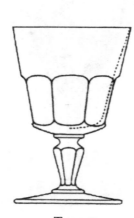

Texas
Baccarat

Piccadilly
Baccarat

Buckingham
Baccarat

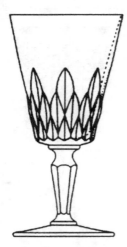

Carcassonne
Baccarat

Turin
Baccarat

Renaissance
Baccarat

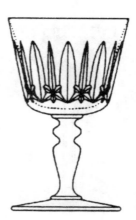

Isle de France
Baccarat

Armagnac
Baccarat

14

Alsace
Baccarat

Austerlitz
Baccarat

Juvisy
Baccarat

Chef D'Oeuvre
Baccarat

Harcourt
Baccarat

Ems
Baccarat
Gold Trim

Empire
Baccarat
Gold Design & Trim

Polignac
Baccarat

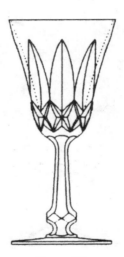

Tourville
Baccarat

Colbert
Baccarat

BAC 1
Baccarat
Pressed

Odeon
Baccarat

Passy
Baccarat

Lucullus
Baccarat

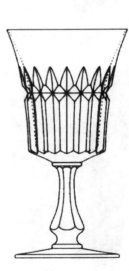

Navarre
Baccarat

Monaco
Baccarat

D'Assas
Baccarat

Narcisse
Baccarat

Massena
Baccarat

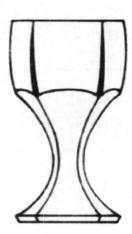

Mercure
Baccarat

Neptune
Baccarat
Champagne Flute

Athena
Baccarat

Charmes
Baccarat

Orion
Baccarat
Barware

Pluton
Baccarat
Barware

Rotary
Baccarat
Barware

Consul
Barthmann

King Richard
Barthmann

Liege
Barthmann

Melodie
Barthmann

Americana
Bayel
Pressed

Antoinette
Bayel

Bacchante
Bayel
Frosted Stem

Baquette
Bayel

Bordeaux
Bayel

Dominique
Bayel

Josephine
Bayel

Lafayette
Bayel

Lille
Bayel

Napoleon
Bayel
Frosted Stem

Normandy
Bayel

Orleans
Bayel

Owl
Bayel
Frosted Stem

Palais
Bayel
Gold Design

Paris Rose
Bayel

17

Sea Horse
Bayel
Frosted Stem

Strasbourg
Bayel

Strawberry Diamond
Bayel

Trianon
Bayel

Venus
Bayel

BFC 1
Blefeld & Co. (Cordial)
Gray Cut, Platinum Trim

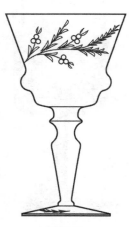

BFC 2
Blefeld & Co.

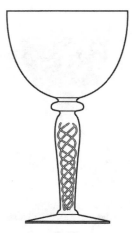

Swirlette
Blefeld & Co.

Airtwist
Block

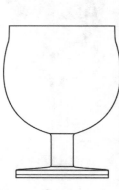

Capers
Block

Chateau Blanc
Block

Chateau D'Argent
Block
Platinum Trim

Chateau D'Or
Block
Gold Trim

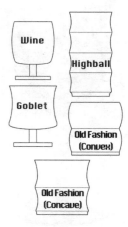

Chromatics
Block
Various Colors

Cote D'Argent
Block
Platinum Trim

España
Block
Blanco (clear), Noche (smoke)

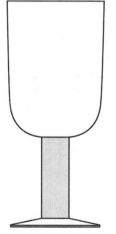

Floral
Block
Green Stem

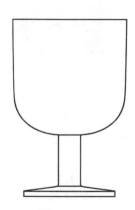

Harmony
Block

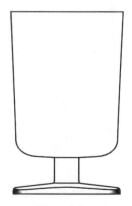

Transition
Block
Square Foot

Tulipa
Block
Various Colors

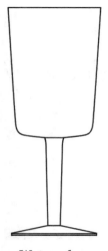

Watercolors
Block
Various Colors

BOC 1
Bohemia

BOC 2
Bohemia
Multicolored

BOC 3
Bohemia
Gold Trim

BOC 4
Bohemia

BOC 5
Bohemia

21-660
Bohemia

Belaire
Bohemia
Air Twist

Belfast
Bohemia

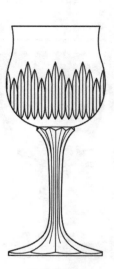

Brighton
Bohemia

19

Edinburg
Bohemia

Isabelle
Bohemia

Lada
Bohemia

Marquis
Bohemia

Pinwheel
Bohemia

Queen's Lace
Bohemia
Gold Trim

Riviera
Bohemia

Simone
Bohemia

Stratford
Bohemia

Sydney
Bohemia

Lisa
Borgfeldt
Also Optic and Colored

Lorraine
Brodegaard

1041-1
Bryce

Governor
Bryce
1041, Cut 206

Tulip
Bryce
1041

Mode
Bryce
10A, Cut Stem

Cretan
Bryce
13A, Engr. 1100

Fern Leaf
Bryce
13A, Cut 290

Festival
Bryce
13A, Cut 293 ½

Kingsley
Bryce
13A, Cut 298

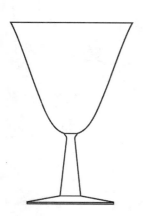

Simplicity
Bryce
13A, Clear or Milk Glass

Etch 410
Bryce
355

Laurel
Bryce
355, Cut 790

Etch 327
Bryce
300

St. Regis
Bryce
240, Gold Band 35

Candlelight
Bryce
30A, Cut 363

Ballet
Bryce
1042

Minuet
Bryce
1037

Adonis
Bryce
1045

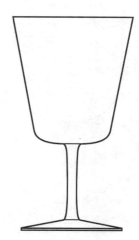

Homestead
Bryce
19A

Band 600
Bryce
285, Sand Blasted

Laurel
Bryce
285, Cut 790

Cut 887
Bryce
460

Andora
Bryce
978, Cut 117

Flora
Bryce
978, Cut 241

Stem 350
Bryce

Etch 375
Bryce
350

Laurel
Bryce
350, Cut 790

Modern Classic
Bryce
15A, Cut Stem

943-1
Bryce

Colonnade
Bryce
943, Cut Stem

Columbine
Bryce
943

771-1
Bryce

Columbine
Bryce
Twisted Stem

Stem 325
Bryce

785-1
Bryce

Cascade
Bryce
785, Gray Cutting

Harvest
Bryce
6A, Cut 267 ½

Pendant
Bryce
6A, Brown Bowl

Wreath
Bryce
6A, Cut 278

Princess
Bryce
29A, Cut 374, Platinum

Vine
Bryce
29A, Cut 269

Essex
Bryce

Bridal Wreath
Bryce
12A, Cut 17A

Celeste
Bryce
12A, Cut 294 ½

Heritage
Bryce
4A, Cut Stem

Snowflower
Bryce
16A, Cut 299

Stem 20A
Bryce

Lenox
Bryce
20A, Cut 323

235-1
Bryce

Stem 942
Bryce

Lace
Bryce
942, Etch 515

Prince Consort
Bryce
942, Cut 1A

942-1
Bryce

942-2
Bryce

Old Lace
Bryce
784, Band 567

784-1
Bryce

784-2
Bryce

784-3
Bryce

784-4
Bryce

784-5
Bryce

865-1
Bryce

865-2
Bryce

Exquisite
Bryce
866, Platinum Trim

Van Wyck
Bryce
866

866-1
Bryce

866-2
Bryce

866-3
Bryce

798-1
Bryce

Autumn
Bryce
1A, Cut 267 ½

Symphony
Bryce
1A

Woodflower
Bryce
1A, Cut 266

Stem 7A
Bryce

Debut
Bryce
7A

Debut
Bryce
7A, Gold or Platinum

Rowena
Bryce
7A, Cut 279

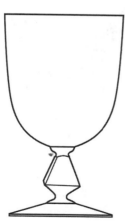

Aquarius
Bryce
961

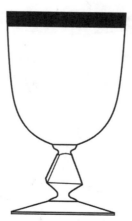

Aquarius
Bryce
961, Platinum Trim

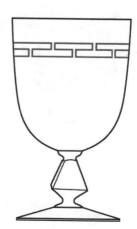

Cretan
Bryce
961

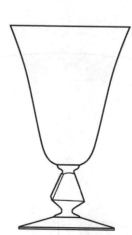

Tulip Aquarius
Bryce
963, Cut Stem

Hellenic
Bryce
934

934-1
Bryce
Platinum Trim

Wilmington
Bryce
945

945-1
Bryce

8A-1
Bryce

Sharon
Bryce
8A

Starburst
Bryce
8A, Cut 283

Stem 894
Bryce

895-1
Bryce

Stem 896
Bryce

896-1
Bryce

Spring Flower
Bryce
22A, Cut 388 ½

Roslyn
Bryce
26A, Plain or Platinum

Ardmore
Bryce
27A, Cut 383

Wales
Bryce
682/949

Wales Laurel
Bryce
682, Cut 790

Empire
Bryce
949, Cut 7X

Mayfair
Bryce
949, Cut 319

Traditional
Bryce
949, Cut 552C

Antique
Bryce
1147, Colors

Kildare
Bryce
954

Stem 657
Bryce

Apollo
Bryce
925

Stem 886
Bryce

886-1
Bryce

Contour
Bryce
869

Tulip
Bryce
Sawtooth Design

Delhi
Bryce
946

Brilliant
Bryce
740, Cut 265

Colonial
Bryce
740, Cut 21A

Early American
Bryce
740

Early American Laurel
Bryce
740, Cut 790

White House
Bryce
740, Cut 65

740-1
Bryce

740-2
Bryce

740-3
Bryce

BRY 1
Bryce

Stem 628
Bryce

638-1
Bryce

638-2
Bryce

761-1
Bryce

Fern Leaf
Bryce
854

854-1
Bryce

854-2
Bryce

854-3
Bryce

Stem 731
Bryce

Springtime
Bryce
688

688-1
Bryce
Ruby Bowl, Etched

688-2
Bryce

Concord
Bryce
862

Williamsburg
Bryce
862, Cut 167

Georgian
Bryce
575

575-1
Bryce

Aristocrat
Bryce
850

Betsy Ross
Bryce
880

Wakefield
Bryce
879, Cut 178

879-1
Bryce

625-1
Bryce

Lido
Bryce
2A

Tempo
Bryce
5A

Modern
Bryce
761

Futura
Bryce
1050

El Rancho
Bryce
1137

Holiday
Bryce
1139

Turkey Eagle
Bryce
1102 1/4, Barware

Cambridge Shapes and Lines

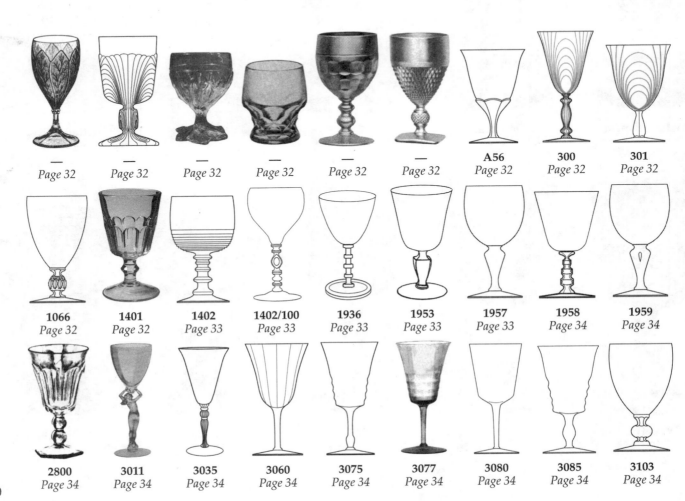

| | | | | | | A56 | 300 | 301 |
| *Page 32* | *Page 32* | *Page 32* | *Page 32* | *Page 32* | *Page 32* | *Page 32* | *Page 32* | *Page 32* |

1066
Page 32

1401
Page 32

1402
Page 33

1402/100
Page 33

1936
Page 33

1953
Page 33

1957
Page 33

1958
Page 34

1959
Page 34

2800
Page 34

3011
Page 34

3035
Page 34

3060
Page 34

3075
Page 34

3077
Page 34

3080
Page 34

3085
Page 34

3103
Page 34

3104
Page 35

3106
Page 35

3109
Page 35

3111
Page 35

3112
Page 35

3114
Page 35

3115
Page 35

3116
Page 35

3118
Page 36

3120
Page 36

3121
Page 36

3122
Page 36

3123
Page 36

3124
Page 36

3126
Page 37

3130
Page 37

3132
Page 38

3134
Page 38

3135
Page 38

3138
Page 38

3139
Page 38

3143
Page 38

3144
Page 39

3400
Page 39

3500
Page 39

3575
Page 39

3600
Page 40

3625
Page 40

3650
Page 40

3675
Page 40

3700
Page 40

3725
Page 41

3750
Page 41

3775
Page 41

3776
Page 42

3777
Page 42

3778
Page 42

3779
Page 42

3790
Page 43

3795
Page 43

3797
Page 43

3798
Page 43

3900
Page 44

4000
Page 44

5000
Page 44

7606
Page 44

7801
Page 44

7858
Page 44

7966
Page 44

7967
Page 44

Arcadia
Cambridge

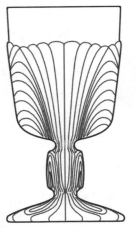

Caprice
Cambridge
Pressed

Everglade
Cambridge

Georgian
Cambridge
Pressed

Martha Washington
Cambridge
Pressed

Mount Vernon
Cambridge

Roses
Cambridge
A56, Cut 2P

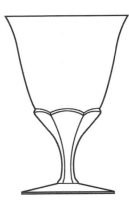

Today
Cambridge
A56, Clear

Caprice
Cambridge
300

Alpine
Cambridge
300, Frosted Stem/Foot

Caprice
Cambridge
301

Aurora
Cambridge
1066

1066
Cambridge
1066, Gold Trim

Diane
Cambridge
1066, Etch 752

Jefferson
Cambridge
1401, Pressed

Tally Ho
Cambridge
1402

Tally Ho
Cambridge
1402/100

Dec. 1007-8
Cambridge
1402/100, Gold Design

Minerva
Cambridge
1402/100

Valencia
Cambridge
1402/100

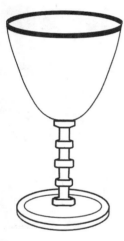

Dec. 450
Cambridge
1936, Gold Band

Killarney
Cambridge
1936, Cut 920

Neo Classic
Cambridge
1936, Cut 907

The Pines
Cambridge
1936, Cut 919

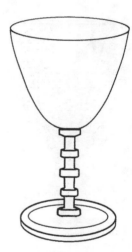

Pristine
Cambridge
1936

Cathedral
Cambridge
1953

Joan of Arc
Cambridge
1953, Cut 1082

Old English
Cambridge
1953, Cut 10

Silver Wheat
Cambridge
1953

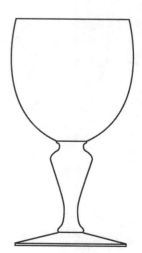

Sonata
Cambridge
1957

Radiant Rose
Cambridge
1958

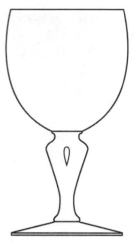

Doric
Cambridge
1959, Air Bubble in Stem

Colonial
Cambridge
2800

Nude Stem
Cambridge
3011

Apple Blossom
Cambridge
3011, Etch 744

Stem 3035
Cambridge

Lorna
Cambridge
3035, Etch 748

Etch 703
Cambridge
3060

Etch 704
Cambridge
3060

Etch 704
Cambridge
3075

Stem 3077
Cambridge

Cleo
Cambridge
3077

Chantilly
Cambridge
3080

Imperial Hunt Scene
Cambridge
3085, Etch 718

Stem 3103
Cambridge

Stem 3104
Cambridge

Laurel Wreath
Cambridge
3106

Lily of the Valley
Cambridge
3106

Rose Point
Cambridge
3106

Vintage
Cambridge
3109

Wedding Band
Cambridge
3109, Gold Dec. 460

Stem 3111
Cambridge

Candlelight
Cambridge
3111

Elaine
Cambridge
3111

Ye Olde Ivy
Cambridge
3112

Candlelight
Cambridge
3114

3114-1
Cambridge
Cut Candlelight

Rosalie
Cambridge
3115, Etch 731

Candlelight
Cambridge
3116, Cut 897

Lucia
Cambridge
3116, Cut 824

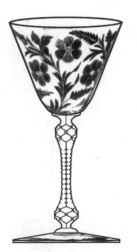

Carnation
Cambridge
3118, Cut 732

Stem 3120
Cambridge

3120-1
Cambridge

Apple Blossom
Cambridge
3120, Etch 744

Stem 3121
Cambridge

Achilles
Cambridge
3121, Cut 698

Elaine
Cambridge
3121

Portia
Cambridge
3121

Rose Point
Cambridge
3121

Wildflower
Cambridge
3121

Stem 3122
Cambridge

Diane
Cambridge
3122, Etch 752

Portia
Cambridge
3122

Aero Optic
Cambridge
3123

Stem 3124
Cambridge

Apple Blossom
Cambridge
3124, Etch 744

Gloria
Cambridge
3124, Etch 746

Portia
Cambridge
3124

Stem 3126
Cambridge

Elaine
Cambridge
3126

Portia
Cambridge
3126

Valencia
Cambridge
3126

Stem 3130
Cambridge

Apple Blossom
Cambridge
3130, Etch 744

Cordelia
Cambridge
3130, Cut 812

Etch 739
Cambridge
3130

Glendale
Cambridge
3130, Cut 1028

Gloria
Cambridge
3130, Etch 746

Portia
Cambridge
3130

Rosalie
Cambridge
3130, Etch 731

Wedding Rose
Cambridge
3130, Cut 998

Belfast
Cambridge
3132, Cut 942

Mansard
Cambridge
3132, Cut 906

Broadmoor
Cambridge
3134, Cut 951

Apple Blossom
Cambridge
3135, Etch 744

Chantilly
Cambridge
3138

Carnation
Cambridge
3138, Cut 732

Juliana
Cambridge
3139, Cut 997

King George
Cambridge
3139, Cut 1027

Laurel Wreath
Cambridge
3139

Maryland
Cambridge
3139, Cut 985

Sicily
Cambridge
3139, Cut 984

Triumph
Cambridge
3139, Platinum Trim

Wedding Band
Cambridge
3139, Gold Dec. 460

Gyro Optic
Cambridge
3143

Virginian
Cambridge
3144

Stem 3400
Cambridge

Gadroon
Cambridge
3500

Adonis
Cambridge
3500, Cut 720

Croesus
Cambridge
3500, Cut 722

Elaine
Cambridge
3500

Minerva
Cambridge
3500

Rose Point
Cambridge
3500

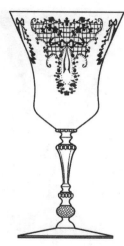

Valencia
Cambridge
3500

Victory Wreath
Cambridge
3500, Cut 723

Celestial
Cambridge
3575, Cut 930

Diane
Cambridge
3575, Etch 752

Portia
Cambridge
3575

Regency
Cambridge
3575

Symphony
Cambridge
3575, Cut 929

Chantilly
Cambridge
3600

Chantilly
Cambridge
3625

Astoria
Cambridge
3650, Gold Trim

Blossom Time
Cambridge
3675

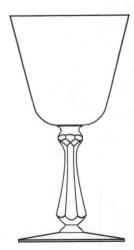

Dunkirk
Cambridge
3700

Ardsley
Cambridge
3700, Cut 1005

Cambridge Rose
Cambridge
3700, Cut 1074

Chesterfield
Cambridge
3700

King Edward
Cambridge
3700, Cut 821

Laurel Wreath
Cambridge
3700

Manor
Cambridge
3700, Cut 1003

Montrose
Cambridge
3700, Cut 1004

Strathmore
Cambridge
3700, Cut 1006

Tempo
Cambridge
3700, Cut 1029

Wedding Band
Cambridge
3700, Gold Dec. 460

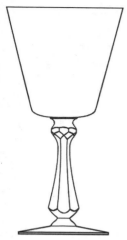

Castleton
Cambridge
3725

Bijou
Cambridge
3725, Cut 1011

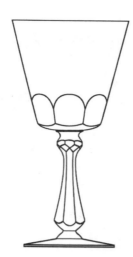

Cadet
Cambridge
3725

Plaza
Cambridge
3725, Cut 1018

Star
Cambridge
3725, Cut 1016

Wildflower
Cambridge
3725

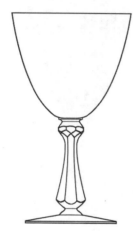

Charleston
Cambridge
3750

Bexley
Cambridge
3750, Cut 1014

Euclid
Cambridge
3750, Cut 1017

Fuchsia
Cambridge
3750, Cut 1019

Hanover
Cambridge
3750, Cut 1015

Harvest
Cambridge
3750, Cut 1053

Ivy
Cambridge
3750, Cut 1059

Minton Wreath
Cambridge
3750, Cut 1012

Arlington
Cambridge
3775

Chantilly
Cambridge
3775

Roxbury
Cambridge
3775, Cut 1030

Candlelight
Cambridge
3776

Dover
Cambridge
3776, Cut 1034

Garland
Cambridge
3776, Cut 1044

Maryland
Cambridge
3776, Cut 985

Minuet
Cambridge
3776, Cut 990

Shelburne
Cambridge
3776

Patrician
Cambridge
3777, Cut 1035

Southgate
Cambridge
3777, Cut 1045

Winsor
Cambridge
3777

Century
Cambridge
3778

Deerfield
Cambridge
3778, Cut 1033

Chantilly
Cambridge
3779

Daffodil
Cambridge
3779

Roselyn
Cambridge
3779

Autumn
Cambridge
3790, Cut 1092

Festoon
Cambridge
3790, Cut 1071

Flight
Cambridge
3790, Cut 3P

Lily of the Valley
Cambridge
3790, Cut 1069

Lynbrook
Cambridge
3790, Cut 1070

Magnolia
Cambridge
3790

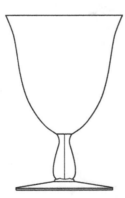

Simplicity
Cambridge
3790

Starburst
Cambridge
3790, Cut 4P

Starlite
Cambridge
3790, Cut 10P

Victory
Cambridge
3790, Platinum Trim

Sweetheart
Cambridge
3795

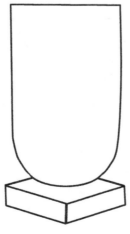

Cambridge Square
Cambridge
3797

Cambridge Square
Cambridge
3798

Triumph
Cambridge
3798, Platinum Trim

Corinth
Cambridge
3900

Cascade
Cambridge
4000

Heirloom
Cambridge
5000, Pressed

Cleo
Cambridge
7606

Marjorie
Cambridge
7606

Chantilly
Cambridge
7801

Martha
Cambridge
7858

Apple Blossom
Cambridge
7966, Gold Dec. 1036

Bacchus
Cambridge
7966

Lexington
Cambridge
7966, Cut 758

Rondo
Cambridge
7966, Cut 1081

Talisman Rose
Cambridge
7966, Gold Dec. 1063

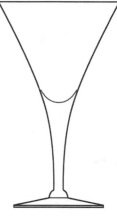

Trumpet
Cambridge
7966

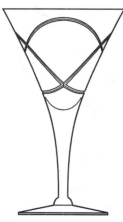

Wedding Rings
Cambridge
7966

Melody
Cambridge
7967

Chantilly
Carico
Optic

Danse de Feu
Cartier

Des Ballets Russes
Cartier

Des Must
Cartier

Des Must de Cartier
Cartier

Du Prince
Cartier

La Maison
Cartier
Champagne Flute

Venitienne
Cartier
Champagne Flute

Cavan
Cavan

Killykeen
Cavan

Shannon
Cavan

Sheelin
Cavan

CEC 1
Celebrity
Gray Bowl

Wedding Band
Celebrity
Platinum Trim

Harding
Central Glass

Morgan
Central Glass
Clear

Morgan
Central Glass
Twisted Stem

Morgan
Central Glass
24, Blue

Veninga
Central Glass

Ascot
Ceska

Brilliance
Ceska
Champagne Flute

Canterbury
Ceska

Concerto
Ceska

Danielle
Ceska

Etude
Ceska

Galaxie
Ceska

Grand Renaissance
Ceska

Helene
Ceska

Prague
Ceska

Regency
Ceska

Solitaire
Ceska
Champagne Flute

Suzanna
Ceska
Champagne Flute

Symphony
Ceska

Tiara
Ceska

Tradition
Ceska

Azure Royal
Christian Dior
Blue Stem, Gold Trim

Bijoux
Christian Dior
Clear, Gold Rings

Casablanca
Christian Dior
Etched

Casablanca
Christian Dior
Black Cat, Gold Accent

Dior Bow
Christian Dior
Frosted Bow

Dior Rose
Christian Dior
Frosted Rose

Ebony Dior
Christian Dior
Black Bowl, Gold Encrusted

Gaudron
Christian Dior
Frosted or Gold Accents

Ligne
Christian Dior

Triomphe
Christian Dior
Gold Trim, Ring, Foot

Colony

COL 1
Colony
Gray Cut Floral

COL 2
Colony
Gray Cut Floral

COL 3
Colony
Clarenbridge Crystal

Airflow
Colony
Spiral Inside Stem

Amaryllis
Colony
Various Colored Stems

Aurora
Colony
Clarenbridge Crystal

Bijoux
Colony
Rainbow Colors

Bon Vivant
Colony

Brigitte
Colony

Chantilly
Colony

Chateau
Colony

Claridge
Colony

Color Crown
Colony
Solid Colors

Consara
Colony

Danube
Colony
Gray Cut Floral

Harvest
Colony
Milk Glass

Imperial
Colony

Joy
Colony
Optic

Kilkenny
Colony
Clarenbridge Crystal

Lily of the Valley
Colony
Cut Floral

Monet
Colony

Neel
Colony
Various Colors

Park Lane
Colony

Provincial
Colony

Regency Ruby
Colony
Red Bowl, Twisted Stem

Retrospect
Colony

Ruby Crown
Colony
Ruby Flashed

Sara
Colony

Saturn
Colony
Red Bowl, Twisted Stem

Strata
Colony
Gold Band on Bowl

Whitehall
Colony
Various Colors

Lady Hamilton
Community

Air Twist
Corcoran

Ardene
Corcoran

Greta
Corcoran

Ingrid
Corcoran
Gold, Platinum, or Plain

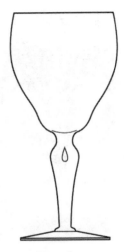

Teardrop
Corcoran
Clear or Smoke

Alicia
Cristal d'Arques/Durand

Clarisse
Cristal d'Arques/Durand
Plain or with Gold Trim

Elise
Cristal d'Arques/Durand

Juliette
Cristal d'Arques/Durand

Lara
Cristal d'Arques/Durand

Emerald
Cristal d'Arques/Durand
"Luminarc" Line, Green Stem

Nocturne
Cristal d'Arques/Durand
Black Stem, France

Rose
Cristal d'Arques/Durand
"Luminarc" Line, Pink Stem

Signature
Cristal d'Arques/Durand
"Luminarc" Line, Colored

Farandole
Cristal d'Arques/Durand
Montelimar Shape

Junon
Cristal d'Arques/Durand
Montelimar Shape

Spirale Mate
Cristal d'Arques/Durand
Montelimar Shape

Esterele
Cristal d'Arques/Durand
Vicomte Shape

Juan
Cristal d'Arques/Durand
Vicomte Shape

Vicomte
Cristal d'Arques/Durand

Capella
Cristal d'Arques/Durand
Plain or with Gold Trim

Diamant
Cristal d'Arques/Durand
Megeve Shape

Feuille
Cristal d'Arques/Durand
Megeve Shape

Pistil
Cristal d'Arques/Durand
Megeve Shape

Castel
Cristal d'Arques/Durand

Grand Vignoble
Cristal d'Arques/Durand

Octime
Cristal d'Arques/Durand
aka "Temptation"

Americana
Cristal d'Arques/Durand
Luminarc- Blue, Clear, or Pink

51

Regency
Cristal d'Arques/Durand

Diamant
Cristal d'Arques/Durand
"Luminarc" Line

Fleury
Cristal d'Arques/Durand
Twisted Stem

Nemours
Cristal d'Arques/Durand
Optic, Twisted Stem

Florence
Cristal d'Arques/Durand
Frosted Petals

Uzes Satine
Cristal d'Arques/Durand
Frosted Stem

Chateauneuf
Cristal d'Arques/Durand

Penelope
Cristal d'Arques/Durand
Nimes Shape

Saphir taille Lance
Cristal d'Arques/Durand
Sapphire Stem

Washington
Cristal d'Arques/Durand

Altesse
Cristal d'Arques/Durand

Antique
Cristal d'Arques/Durand

Dauphine
Cristal d'Arques/Durand

Chateaudun
Cristal d'Arques/Durand

Chantilly
Cristal d'Arques/Durand

Chantilly taille Beaugency
Cristal d'Arques/Durand

Combourg
Cristal d'Arques/Durand

Saumur
Cristal d'Arques/Durand

Versailles
Cristal d'Arques/Durand

CRA 1
Cristal d'Arques/Durand

Cannes
Cristal d'Arques/Durand

St. Maxime
Cristal d'Arques/Durand

Meridien
Cristal d'Arques/Durand
"Luminarc" Line

St. Germain
Cristal d'Arques/Durand

Matignon
Cristal d'Arques/Durand
Etched

Flamenco
Cristal d'Arques/Durand

Palmes
Cristal d'Arques/Durand

Flammes
Cristal d'Arques/Durand
"Luminarc" Line

Chaumont
Cristal d'Arques/Durand

Orsay
Cristal d'Arques/Durand

Bengale
Cristal d'Arques/Durand
"Luminarc" Line

Chambery
Cristal d'Arques/Durand

Fontenay
Cristal d'Arques/Durand

Deauville
Cristal d'Arques/Durand
Lude Shape

Lavandou
Cristal d'Arques/Durand
Lude Shape

Lude Lilas
Cristal d'Arques/Durand
Plain Bowl, Purple Stem

St. Cloud
Cristal d'Arques/Durand
Lude Shape

Longchamp
Cristal d'Arques/Durand

Auteuil
Cristal d'Arques/Durand
"Auteuil Lilas," Purple Stem

Avignon
Cristal d'Arques/Durand

Elysee Taille
Cristal d'Arques/Durand

Valencay
Cristal d'Arques/Durand
Plain or with Gold Trim

Ancenis
Cristal d'Arques/Durand

Chenonceaux
Cristal d'Arques/Durand

Palais
Cristal d'Arques/Durand

Ales
Cristal d'Arques/Durand
Villiers shape

Beaulieu
Cristal d'Arques/Durand
Villiers shape

Ventoux
Cristal d'Arques/Durand
Etched, Gold Trim

Villeneuve
Cristal d'Arques/Durand

Onyx
Cristal d'Arques/Durand
Black Stem

Chantelle
Cristal d'Arques/Durand

Fontainebleau
Cristal d'Arques/Durand

Dampierre
Cristal d'Arques/Durand
Etched

Annecy
Cristal d'Arques/Durand

Rosaline
Cristal d'Arques/Durand
Pink

Diamond
Cristal d'Arques/Durand

Louvre
Cristal d'Arques/Durand

Tuilleries/Villandry
Cristal d'Arques/Durand

Rambouillet
Cristal d'Arques/Durand

Paris Royal
Cristal d'Arques/Durand

Vendome taille Lance
Cristal d'Arques/Durand

Vendome Uni
Cristal d'Arques/Durand

Pompadour
Cristal d'Arques/Durand

Bretagne
Cristal d'Arques/Durand

Petale
Cristal d'Arques/Durand

Tornade
Cristal d'Arques/Durand

Artic
Cristal d'Arques/Durand
"Arcoroc" Line

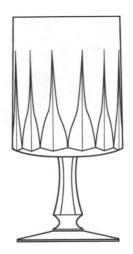

Bedford
Cristal d'Arques/Durand

Monceaux
Cristal d'Arques/Durand
Optic

Cheverny
Cristal d'Arques/Durand
Barware

Amboise
Cristal d'Arques/Durand
Plain Barware

Fascination
Cristal de Flandre

Albinoni
Cristal de Sevres

Keos/Beaubourg
Cristal de Sevres

Niagara
Cristal de Sevres

Norma
Cristal de Sevres

Primavera
Cristal de Sevres
Frosted Design

Ritz
Cristal de Sevres
Gold Trim, Optic

Savannah
Cristal de Sevres

Sologne
Cristal de Sevres
Gold Trim

Titien
Cristal de Sevres
Optic

Watteau
Cristal de Sevres

Celine
Crystal Clear Industries

Valerie
Crystal Clear Industries
Frosted Colored Stem

Monaco
Crystal Import Corp.

Atlas
Czechoslovakia
Various Colors, Gold Trim

Flair
Czechoslovakia

Pinwheel
Czechoslovakia

Camilla
Da Vinci

DHC 1
Daniel Hechter
Colored Stem

Dansk

Adrianna
Dansk

Advent
Dansk
Barware

Alborg
Dansk

Althea
Dansk
6 Sided Stem

Anna
Dansk

Annalise
Dansk

Baguette
Dansk
Barware

Belle
Dansk

Bistro
Dansk

Carla
Dansk

Christina
Dansk

Cloud
Dansk
Barware

Elegant
Dansk

Erika
Dansk

Facette
Dansk
Round Facetted Base

Felicia
Dansk

Flora
Dansk
Cordial

Fredericia
Dansk

Genna
Dansk

Greta
Dansk

Gustav
Dansk

Hanna
Dansk

Holsted
Dansk

Julien
Dansk

Karin
Dansk

Keri
Dansk

Kirsten
Dansk

Kolby
Dansk

Lisa
Dansk

Melon
Dansk
Barware

Mesa
Dansk

Michel
Dansk

Neptune
Dansk

Nicole
Dansk

Oval Facette
Dansk
Oval Facetted Base

Pia
Dansk

Rienna
Dansk

Scroll
Dansk
Barware

Simplicity
Dansk

Swirl
Dansk
Barware

Tapestries
Dansk

Tivoli
Dansk

Ursula
Dansk

Agatha
Dartington

Chateau
Dartington

Chateauneuf
Dartington

Chelsea
Dartington

Rachael
Dartington

Rummer
Dartington

Sharon
Dartington

Beaune
Daum

Bolero
Daum

Arabesque
Denby
Various Colors

Aurora
Denby
Various Colors

Carousel
Denby
Various Colors

Chamonix
Denby
Various Colors

Chateau
Denby
Colored Bowl

Exeter
Denby

Flare
Denby
Various Colors

Frederick
Denby

Guildford
Denby

Gustav
Denby

Mirage
Denby
Various Colors

Moonrise
Denby
Various Colors

Olympia
Denby
Various Colors

Reflections
Denby

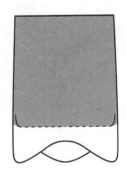

Skol
Denby
Various Colors, Barware

Stirling
Denby

Washington
Denby

Blue Lustre
Dorothy Thorpe
Blue Iridescent

Bubble
Dorothy Thorpe
Clear Iridescent

Gold Dot
Dorothy Thorpe

Gold Fleck
Dorothy Thorpe

Golden Band
Dorothy Thorpe

Hydrangea
Dorothy Thorpe
Lilac Stem

Silver Band
Dorothy Thorpe

Topaz Lustre
Dorothy Thorpe
Golden Iridescent

Royal
Doyen
Various Colored Bowls

Mardis Gras
Duncan
42, Pressed

Shell & Tassel
Duncan
555, Pressed

Georgian
Duncan
103, Pressed

Carribean
Duncan
112, Pressed

Kimberly
Duncan
22, Ruby Flashed

Hobnail
Duncan
118, Pressed

Flair
Duncan
150

Canterbury
Duncan
115, Pressed

Three Faces
Duncan
400, Pressed

Sandwich
Duncan
41

Waterford
Duncan
102, Pressed

Kohinoor
Duncan
5322, Cut 690

Sun Ray
Duncan
5322, Cut 691

Belfast
Duncan, Square Base
5323, Cut 734

Killarney
Duncan, Square Base
5323, Cut 686

Virginia Dare
Duncan, Square Base
5323, Cut 703

Clematis
Duncan
5330

Dover
Duncan
5330

Magnolia
Duncan
5330

Nobility
Duncan
5330, Cut 775

Ruby
Duncan
5330

Saratoga
Duncan
5330, Cut 769

Sheffield
Duncan
5330, Cut 768

Chartreuse
Duncan
5333, Green

Spiral Flutes
Duncan
40

Bristol Diamond
Duncan
32, Cut 803

Chesterfield
Duncan
32, Cut 717

Sherwood
Duncan
32, Cut 645

32-1
Duncan
32

Duncan Rose
Duncan
D8

Ethereal
Duncan
D8

Patio
Duncan
D8 or 5152

Starlight
Duncan
D8

Azalea
Duncan
5115, Cut 694

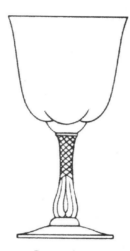

Canterbury
Duncan
5115, Blown Stem

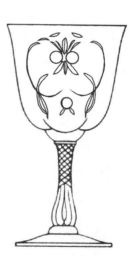

Chantilly
Duncan
5115, Cut 773

Maytime
Duncan
5115, Cut 698

Phoebus
Duncan
5115, Cut 621

Remembrance
Duncan
5115

Tripole
Duncan (Wine)
5115, Cut 750

Tristan
Duncan
5115, Cut 622

Alhambra
Duncan
504, Cut 607

Granada
Duncan
504

Stratford
Duncan
504, Cut 689

Adoration
Duncan
5321

Tiara
Duncan
5321, Cut 683

Trianon
Duncan
5321

Burgundy
Duncan
5326, Cut 777

Deauville
Duncan
5326

Francis First
Duncan
5326, Cut 783

Indian Tree
Duncan
5326

Charmaine Rose
Duncan
5375

Diamond
Duncan
5375

Garland
Duncan
5375

Monterey
Duncan
5375, Cut 697

Queen's Lace
Duncan
5375

Andover
Duncan
5329, Cut 760

Eternally Yours
Duncan
5331, Cut 765

Language of Flowers
Duncan
5331

Victory
Duncan
5331

Royal Lace
Duncan
5301

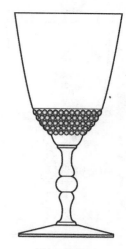

Teardrop
Duncan
5301

Bridal Bow
Duncan
503, Cut 782

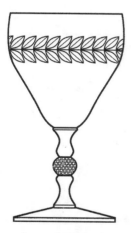

Laurel Wreath
Duncan
503, Cut 640

Touraine
Duncan
503

503-1
Duncan
503

First Love
Duncan
5111 ½

Royal Lace
Duncan
5111 ½

Terrace
Duncan
5111 ½

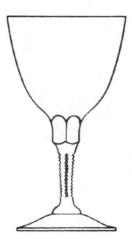

Coronation
Duncan
D13

Heritage
Duncan
D13

Margaret Rose
Duncan
D13

Duncan

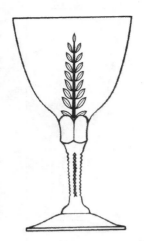

Pine Tree
Duncan
D13

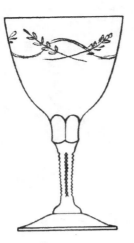

Regency
Duncan
D13

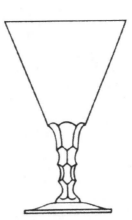

Elegance
Duncan
D15

Rhythm
Duncan
D15

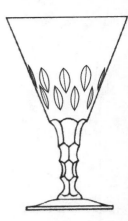

Splendor
Duncan
D15

Marquis
Duncan
D613

Wistaria
Duncan
D613

Tempo
Duncan
D635

Thea
Duncan
D635

Druid
Duncan
D621

Etude
Duncan
D616

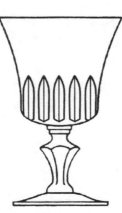

Radcliff
Duncan
D616

St. Charles
Duncan
D616

Athena
Duncan
D1

Fern
Duncan
D1

Governor Clinton
Duncan
D1

Mandarin
Duncan
D1, Gray Greek Key

Spring Glory
Duncan
D1

Coralbel
Duncan
D11

Devon Spray
Duncan
D11

Essex
Duncan
D11

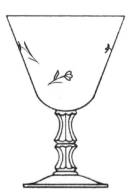

Petite
Duncan
D11

Platinum Band
Duncan
D11

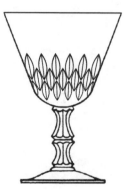

Radiance
Duncan
D11

Simplicity
Duncan
D11

Cathay
Duncan
5317

Dogwood
Duncan
5317

Coronet
Duncan
5317, Cut 682

Juno
Duncan
5317, Cut 688

Deauville
Duncan
D3

Duncan Phyfe
Duncan
D3

Pickwick
Duncan
D3

Reverie
Duncan
D3

Wild Rose
Duncan
D3

Willow
Duncan
D3

Double Wedding
Duncan
D627, Gold and Platinum

Terrace
Duncan
Tiered Stem

Candlelight
Duncan
D2

Mesa
Duncan
D2

Lily of the Valley
Duncan
D4

Lily of the Valley
Duncan
Undecorated, D4

Belvedere
Duncan
D6

Concerto
Duncan
D6

Cretan
Duncan
D5

Dawn
Duncan
D5

Spring Beauty
Duncan
D5

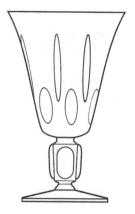

Sundown
Duncan
D7

Countess
Duncan
D612

Carousel
Easterling

Marquise
Easterling

Venetian Star
Easterling

Embassy
Ebeling & Reuss

Emperor
Ebeling & Reuss
Gold Trim

Marchioness
Ebeling & Reuss
Colored Bowl, Gold Trim

Marquis
Ebeling & Reuss
Gold Trim

Mozart
Ebeling & Reuss

Ruby
Ebeling & Reuss

Appin
Edinburgh
T601

Appin
Edinburgh
Cut Stem

Ayr
Edinburgh

Balmoral
Edinburgh

Berkeley
Edinburgh

Duet
Edinburgh

Embassy
Edinburgh

Finesse
Edinburgh

Gleneagles
Edinburgh
85080

Glenshee
Edinburgh
68123

Highland
Edinburgh

Holyrood
Edinburgh
86000

Iona
Edinburgh
81060

Isla
Edinburgh

Kelso
Edinburgh

Lomond
Edinburgh

Lomond
Edinburgh
82016

Montrose
Edinburgh

Rhapsody
Edinburgh

Royal
Edinburgh

Serenade
Edinburgh

Silhouette
Edinburgh

Skye
Edinburgh

Star of Edinburgh
Edinburgh
T335

Stirling
Edinburgh

Sutherland
Edinburgh
81000

Symphony
Edinburgh

Thistle
Edinburgh
H828, Engraved

Thistle
Edinburgh
"blank"

Tweed
Edinburgh

Vienna
Edinburgh

Bridal Rose
Executive House

Empire
Fabergé

73

Foliage
Fabergé

Kissing Doves
Fabergé

Nobilis
Fabergé

Ville de Lyon
Fabergé

Elegance
Fine Arts

Romance of the Stars
Fine Arts

Romance Rose
Fine Arts

Royal Diamond
Fine Arts

Tranquility
Fine Arts

Wildflower
Fine Arts

| 660 | 661 | 766 | 858 | 863 | 867 | 869 | 870 | 877 |
| Page 80 | Page 80 | Page 80 | Page 80 | Page 81 | Page 82 | Page 82 | Page 82 | Page 82 |

| 879 | 880 | 890 | 891 | 892 | 1372 | 1605 | 1630 | 2056 |
| Page 82 | Page 83 | Page 83 | Page 83 | Page 83 | Page 84 | Page 84 | Page 84 | Page 84 |

| 2321 | 2412 | 2449 | 2496 | 2510 | 2620 | 2630 | 2643 | 2700 |
| Page 84 | Page 84 | Page 84 | Page 84 | Page 84 | Page 84 | Page 84 | Page 84 | Page 84 |

| 2713 | 2718 | 2719 | 2770 | 2806 | 2832 | 2860 | 2861 | 2862 |
| Page 85 | Page 85 | Page 85 | Page 85 | Page 85 | Page 85 | Page 85 | Page 85 | Page 85 |

| 2863 | 2882 | 2885 | 2887 | 2903 | 2916 | 2921 | 2934 | 2936 |
| Page 85 | Page 85 | Page 85 | Page 85 | Page 85 | Page 85 | Page 86 | Page 86 | Page 86 |

| 2977 | 2990 | 3013 | 4020 | 4024 | 4161 | 4162 | 4163 | 4180 |
| Page 86 | Page 86 | Page 86 | Page 86 | Page 87 | Page 87 | Page 87 | Page 87 | Page 87 |

Fostoria Shapes and Lines

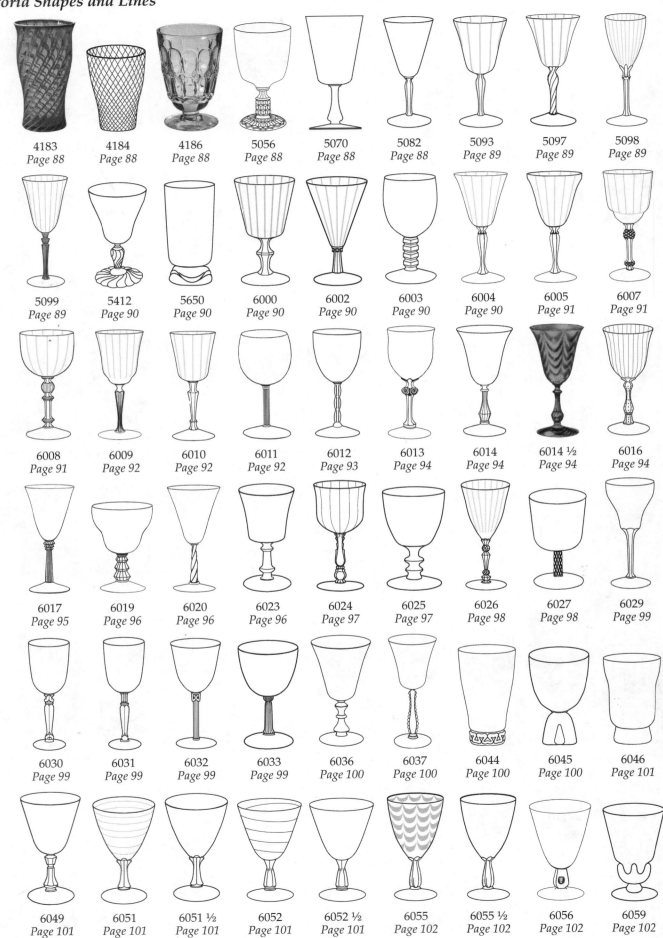

4183 *Page 88*	4184 *Page 88*	4186 *Page 88*	5056 *Page 88*	5070 *Page 88*	5082 *Page 88*	5093 *Page 89*	5097 *Page 89*	5098 *Page 89*
5099 *Page 89*	5412 *Page 90*	5650 *Page 90*	6000 *Page 90*	6002 *Page 90*	6003 *Page 90*	6004 *Page 90*	6005 *Page 91*	6007 *Page 91*
6008 *Page 91*	6009 *Page 92*	6010 *Page 92*	6011 *Page 92*	6012 *Page 93*	6013 *Page 94*	6014 *Page 94*	6014 ½ *Page 94*	6016 *Page 94*
6017 *Page 95*	6019 *Page 96*	6020 *Page 96*	6023 *Page 96*	6024 *Page 97*	6025 *Page 97*	6026 *Page 98*	6027 *Page 98*	6029 *Page 99*
6030 *Page 99*	6031 *Page 99*	6032 *Page 99*	6033 *Page 99*	6036 *Page 100*	6037 *Page 100*	6044 *Page 100*	6045 *Page 100*	6046 *Page 101*
6049 *Page 101*	6051 *Page 101*	6051 ½ *Page 101*	6052 *Page 101*	6052 ½ *Page 101*	6055 *Page 102*	6055 ½ *Page 102*	6056 *Page 102*	6059 *Page 102*

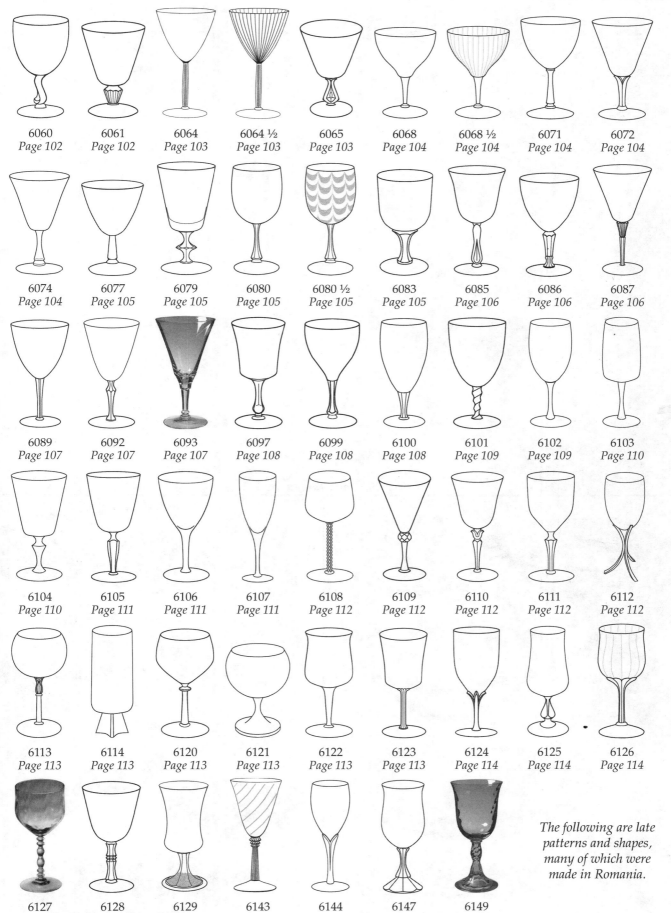

6060	6061	6064	6064 ½	6065	6068	6068 ½	6071	6072
Page 102	*Page 102*	*Page 103*	*Page 103*	*Page 103*	*Page 104*	*Page 104*	*Page 104*	*Page 104*

6074	6077	6079	6080	6080 ½	6083	6085	6086	6087
Page 104	*Page 105*	*Page 105*	*Page 105*	*Page 105*	*Page 105*	*Page 106*	*Page 106*	*Page 106*

6089	6092	6093	6097	6099	6100	6101	6102	6103
Page 107	*Page 107*	*Page 107*	*Page 108*	*Page 108*	*Page 108*	*Page 109*	*Page 109*	*Page 110*

6104	6105	6106	6107	6108	6109	6110	6111	6112
Page 110	*Page 111*	*Page 111*	*Page 111*	*Page 112*	*Page 112*	*Page 112*	*Page 112*	*Page 112*

6113	6114	6120	6121	6122	6123	6124	6125	6126
Page 113	*Page 113*	*Page 113*	*Page 113*	*Page 113*	*Page 113*	*Page 114*	*Page 114*	*Page 114*

6127	6128	6129	6143	6144	6147	6149
Page 114	*Page 114*	*Page 114*	*Page 114*	*Page 115*	*Page 115*	*Page 115*

The following are late patterns and shapes, many of which were made in Romania.

77

Fostoria Shapes and Lines

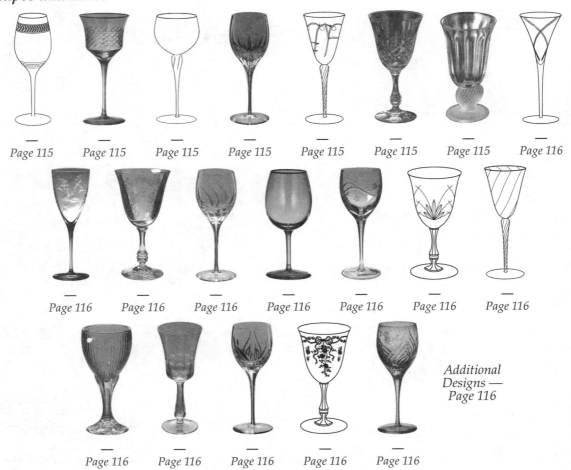

Page 115   *Page 115*   *Page 115*   *Page 115*   *Page 115*   *Page 115*   *Page 115*   *Page 116*

Page 116   *Page 116*   *Page 116*   *Page 116*   *Page 116*   *Page 116*   *Page 116*

Page 116   *Page 116*   *Page 116*   *Page 116*   *Page 116*

Additional Designs — Page 116

Miscellaneous Tableware Lines

"Coronet" Line 2560   *"Fairfax" Line 2375*

"Flame" Line 2545

"Lafayette" Line 2440

"Mayfair" Line 2419

"Pioneer" Line 2350

Mystic
Fostoria
660, Etch 270

Pagoda
Fostoria
660, Etch 90

Washington
Fostoria
660, Etch 266

Woodland
Fostoria
660, Etch 264

Ballet
Fostoria
661, Etch 91

Melrose
Fostoria
661, Etch 268

Orient
Fostoria
661, Etch 265

Virginia
Fostoria
661, Etch 267

766-1
Fostoria
766, Etched, Gold Band

Cascade
Fostoria
766, Gold Dec. 8

Garland
Fostoria
766, Etch 237

Oriental
Fostoria
766, Etch 250

Irish Lace
Fostoria
766, Etch 36

Victory
Fostoria
766, Etch 257

Billow
Fostoria
858, Cut 118

Etch 215
Fostoria
858

Lenore
Fostoria
858, Etch 73

Lily of the Valley
Fostoria
858, Etch 241

New Adam
Fostoria
858, Etch 252

New Vintage
Fostoria
858, Etch 227

Vintage
Fostoria
858, Etch 204

Chrysanthemum
Fostoria
863, Cut 133

Clover
Fostoria
863, Cut 132

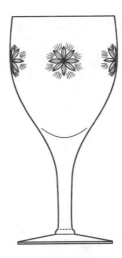

Cut 110
Fostoria
863

Etch 210
Fostoria
863

Etch 212
Fostoria
863

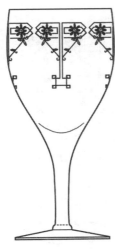

Etch 214
Fostoria
863

Garland
Fostoria
863, Etch 237

Mission
Fostoria
863, Cut 116

New Vintage
Fostoria
863, Etch 227

Persian
Fostoria
863, Etch 253

Small Cloverleaf
Fostoria
863, Etch 67

Parisian
Fostoria
867, Etch 53

Stem 869
Fostoria

Royal
Fostoria
869, Etch 273

Sherman
Fostoria
869, Etch 77

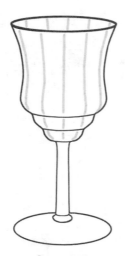

Stem 870
Fostoria

Baronet
Fostoria
870, Etch 92

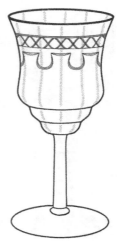

Brunswick
Fostoria
870, Etch 79

Seville
Fostoria
870, Etch 274

Stem 877
Fostoria

Chatteris
Fostoria
877, Cut 197

Oak Leaf
Fostoria
877, Etch 290

Vernon
Fostoria
877, Etch 277

Lily of the Valley
Fostoria
879, Etch 241

Mother of Pearl
Fostoria
879, Iridescent

Garland
Fostoria
880, Etch 237

Kornflower
Fostoria
880, Etch 234

New Vintage
Fostoria
880, Etch 227

Rosilyn
Fostoria
880, Etch 249

Stem 890
Fostoria

Verona
Fostoria
890, Etch 281

Stem 891
Fostoria

Springtime
Fostoria
891, Etch 318

Nordic
Fostoria
892

Ariel
Fostoria
892, Tracing 93

Christine
Fostoria
892, Cut 798

Ingrid
Fostoria
892, Cut 794

Orchid
Fostoria
892, Carving 48

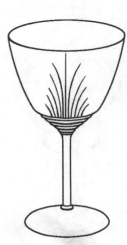

Papyrus
Fostoria
892, Cut 795

Rosemary
Fostoria
892, Etch 339

Coin Glass
Fostoria
1372

Sherwood
Fostoria
1605, Sherbet

Alexis
Fostoria
1630, High Sherbet

American
Fostoria
2056

Priscilla
Fostoria
2321

Colony
Fostoria
2412

Hermitage
Fostoria
2449

Baroque
Fostoria
2496

Sunray
Fostoria
2510

Glacier
Fostoria
2510, Frosted Ribs

Wistar
Fostoria
2620

Century
Fostoria
2630

Holiday
Fostoria
2643

Radiance
Fostoria
2700

Vintage
Fostoria
2713, Milk Glass

Fairmont
Fostoria
2718

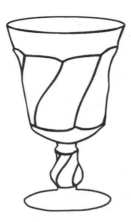

Jamestown
Fostoria
2719, Various Colors

Argus
Fostoria
2770, Various Colors

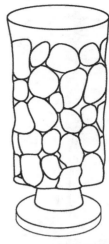

Pebble Beach
Fostoria
2806

Sorrento
Fostoria
2832, Various Colors

Diamond Point
Fostoria
2860

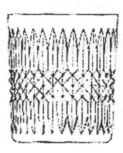

Aspen
Fostoria
2861

Stowe
Fostoria
2862

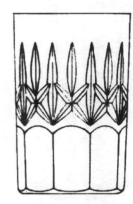

Vail
Fostoria
2863, Cut 925

Moonstone
Fostoria
2882, Various Colors

Stratton
Fostoria
2885

Heritage
Fostoria
2887

Monarch
Fostoria
2903, Heavy Pressed

Fairlane
Fostoria
2916

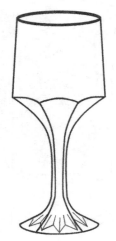

Bracelet
Fostoria
2916, Plat. Dec. 694

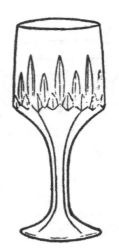

Greenfield
Fostoria
2916, Cut 93

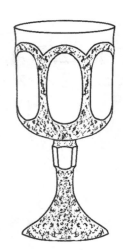

Woodland
Fostoria
2921, Various Colors

York
Fostoria
2934, Barware

Transition
Fostoria
2936

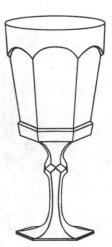

Virginia
Fostoria
2977, Various Colors

Kimberly
Fostoria
2990

Radiance
Fostoria
3013

Stem 4020
Fostoria

Comet
Fostoria
4020, Cut 702

Chelsea
Fostoria
4020, Cut 783

Fern
Fostoria
4020, Etch 305

Formal Garden
Fostoria
4020, Cut 700

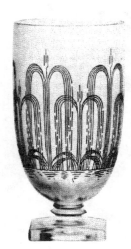

Fountain
Fostoria
4020, Etch 307

Kashmir
Fostoria
4020, Etch 283

Millefleur
Fostoria
4020, Cut 195

Minuet
Fostoria
4020, Etch 285

New Garland
Fostoria
4020, Etch 284

New Yorker
Fostoria
4020, Cut 703

Queen Anne
Fostoria
4020, Etch 306

Rhythm
Fostoria
4020, Cut 773

Tapestry
Fostoria
4020, Cut 701

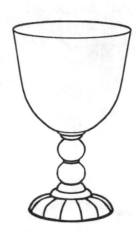

Victorian
Fostoria
4024

Meteor
Fostoria
4024, Cut 726

National
Fostoria
4024, Cut 727

Silver Mist
Fostoria
4024, Frosted

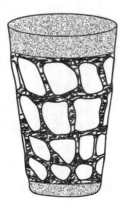

Karnak
Fostoria
4161

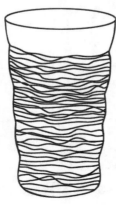

Congo
Fostoria
4162

Inca
Fostoria
4163

Casual Flair
Fostoria
4180, Tumblers

Blue Meadow
Fostoria, Blue
4180, Crystal Print 8

Plain 'n Fancy
Fostoria, Amber
4180, Crystal Print 11

Ring O' Roses
Fostoria, Fawn
4180, Crystal Print 9

Homespun
Fostoria
4183

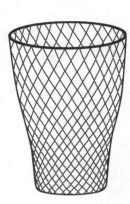

Needlepoint
Fostoria
4184

Mesa
Fostoria
4186

American Lady
Fostoria
5056

Lotus
Fostoria
5070, Etch 232

Poppy/Poupee
Fostoria
5070, Etch 231

Stem 5082/5282
Fostoria

5082-1
Fostoria
5082, Etched Silhouettes

Delphian
Fostoria, Blue Stem
5082, Etch 272

Duchess
Fostoria, Blue Stem
5082, Dec. 51, Gold

Eilene
Fostoria
5082, Etch 83

Richmond
Fostoria
5082, Etch 74

Rogene
Fostoria
5082, Etch 269

Stem 5093/5293
Fostoria

Avalon
Fostoria
5093, Etch 85

Vesper
Fostoria
5093, Etch 275

Stem 5097/5297
Fostoria

5097-1
Fostoria
Etched Design

Beverly
Fostoria
5097, Etch 276

Greek
Fostoria
5097, Etch 45

Spartan
Fostoria
5097, Etch 80

Stem 5098/5298
Fostoria

Acanthus
Fostoria
5098, Etch 282

Berry
Fostoria
5098, Cut 188

Fern
Fostoria
5098, Etch 305

June
Fostoria
5098, Etch 279

Stem 5099/5299
Fostoria

Fostoria

Kashmir
Fostoria
5099, Etch 283

Trojan
Fostoria
5099, Etch 280

Versailles
Fostoria
5099, Etch 278

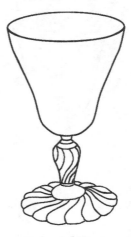

Colonial Dame
Fostoria
5412

Horizon
Fostoria
5650

Stem 6000
Fostoria

Celebrity
Fostoria
6000, Cut 749

Legion
Fostoria
6000, Etch 309

Monroe
Fostoria
6000, Etch 86

Waterbury
Fostoria
6000, Cut 712

Stem 6002/6202
Fostoria

Minuet
Fostoria
6002, Etch 285

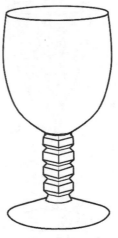

Stem 6003
Fostoria

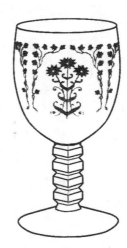

Manor
Fostoria
6003, Etch 286

Stem 6004
Fostoria

Fuchsia
Fostoria
6004, Etch 310

Nairn
Fostoria
6004, Cut 708

Staunton
Fostoria
6004, Cut 707

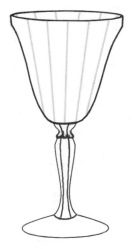

Stem 6005
Fostoria

Florentine
Fostoria
6005, Etch 311

Stem 6007
Fostoria

Bristol
Fostoria
6007, Cut 710

Castle
Fostoria
6007, Etch 87

Eton
Fostoria
6007, Cut 713

Manor
Fostoria
6007, Etch 286

Morning Glory
Fostoria
6007, Etch 313

Oxford
Fostoria
6007, Cut 714

York
Fostoria
6007, Cut 709

Stem 6008
Fostoria

Chateau
Fostoria
6008, Etch 315

Marlboro
Fostoria
6008, Cut 717

Camelot
Fostoria
6009

Doncaster
Fostoria
6009, Cut 718

Grand Majesty
Fostoria
6009, Etched

Midnight Rose
Fostoria
6009, Etch 316

Stem 6010
Fostoria

Sheraton
Fostoria
6010, Etch 317

Wellington
Fostoria
6010, Cut 722

Westminster
Fostoria
6010, Cut 723

Classic
Fostoria
6011, aka "Neo Classic"

Athenian
Fostoria
6011, Cut 770

Directoire
Fostoria
6011, Cut 736

Celestial
Fostoria
6011, Cut 731

Frosted Stem
Fostoria
6011

Mardi Gras
Fostoria
6011, Cut 765

Nectar
Fostoria
6011, Etch 322

Quinfoil
Fostoria
6011, Cut 737

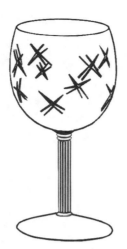

Rocket
Fostoria
6011, Cut 729

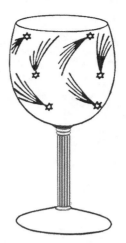

Shooting Stars
Fostoria
6011, Cut 735

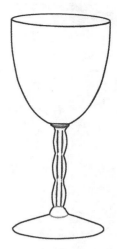

Westchester
Fostoria
6012

Festoon
Fostoria
6012, Cut 738

Heraldry
Fostoria
6012, Cut 43

Ivy
Fostoria
6012, Cut 745

Orbit
Fostoria
6012, Cut 742

Mother of Pearl
Fostoria
6012, Iridescent

Rambler
Fostoria
6012, Etch 323

Regency
Fostoria
6012, Cut 744

Rock Garden
Fostoria
6012, Cut 739

Rondeau
Fostoria
6012, Cut 740

Springtime
Fostoria
6012, Etch 318

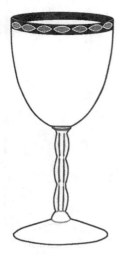

St. Regis
Fostoria
6012, Gold Dec. 616

Watercress
Fostoria
6012, Cut 741

Stem 6013
Fostoria

Allegro
Fostoria
6013, Cut 748

Bouquet
Fostoria
6013, Cut 756

Daisy
Fostoria
6013, Etch 324

Society
Fostoria
6013, Cut 757

Stem 6014
Fostoria

Arcady
Fostoria
6014, Etch 326

Bordeaux
Fostoria
6014, Cut 758

Corsage
Fostoria
6014, Etch 325

Palmetto
Fostoria
6014, Cut 755

Wavecrest
Fostoria
6014 ½

Wilma
Fostoria
6016

6016-1
Fostoria
6016

Meadow Rose
Fostoria
6016, Etch 328

Melba
Fostoria
6016, Cut 761

Navarre
Fostoria
6016, Etch 327

Regis
Fostoria
6016, Gold Dec. 697

Sceptre
Fostoria
6017

Beacon
Fostoria
6017, Cut 767

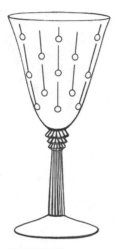

Bridal Shower
Fostoria
6017, Cut 768

Cynthia
Fostoria
6017, Cut 785

Drape
Fostoria
6017, Cut 784

Laurel
Fostoria
6017, Cut 776

Lenox
Fostoria
6017, Etch 330

Lido
Fostoria
6017, Etch 329

Lucerne
Fostoria
6017, Cut 778

Raynel
Fostoria
6017, Cut 777

Ripples
Fostoria
6017, Cut 766

Fostoria

Romance
Fostoria
6017, Etch 341

Shirley
Fostoria
6017, Etch 331

Simplicity
Fostoria
6017, Gold Dec. 618

Rondel
Fostoria
6019

Federal
Fostoria
6019, Cut 771

Laurel
Fostoria
6019, Cut 776

Tulip
Fostoria
6019, Cut 772

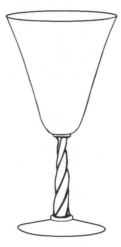

Melody
Fostoria
6020

Gothic
Fostoria
6020, Cut 774

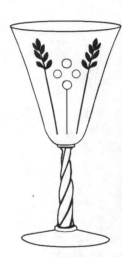

Kimberley
Fostoria
6020, Cut 775

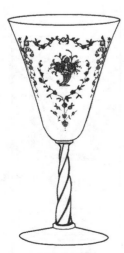

Mayflower
Fostoria
6020, Etch 332

Colfax
Fostoria
6023

Brighton
Fostoria
6023, Cut 801

Cathedral
Fostoria
6023, Cut 792

Chippendale
Fostoria
6023, Cut 788

Colonial Mirror
Fostoria
6023, Etch 334

Dolly Madison
Fostoria
6023, Cut 786

Pilgrim
Fostoria
6023, Cut 787

Revere
Fostoria
6023, Cut 825

Spencerian
Fostoria
6023, Tracing 94

Spire
Fostoria
6023, Cut 793

Wakefield
Fostoria
6023, Cut 820

Willow
Fostoria
6023, Etch 335

Cellini
Fostoria
6024, Loop Optic

Cellini
Fostoria
6024, Regular Optic

Coral Pearl
Fostoria
6024, Iridescent Dec. 623

Regal
Fostoria
6024, Cut 782

Willowmere
Fostoria
6024, Etch 333

Cabot
Fostoria
6025

Hawthorn
Fostoria
6025, Cut 790

Minuet
Fostoria
6025, Cut 826

Plymouth
Fostoria
6025, Etch 336

Sampler
Fostoria
6025, Etch 337

Suffolk
Fostoria
6025, Cut 789

Greenbrier
Fostoria
6026

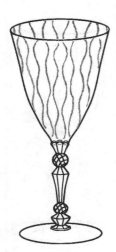

Niagara
Fostoria
6026/2

Chintz
Fostoria
6026, Etch 338

Mulberry
Fostoria
6026, Cut 799

Rheims
Fostoria
6026, Cut 803

Selma
Fostoria
6026, Cut 800

Envoy
Fostoria
6027

Aloha
Fostoria
6027, Cut 805

Cadence
Fostoria
6027, Cut 806

Princess
Fostoria
6027, Cut 824

Salon
Fostoria
6027, Cut 804

Chalice
Fostoria
6029, Cut 812

Saybrooke
Fostoria
6029, Cut 813

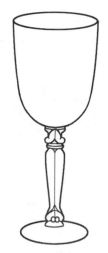

Astrid
Fostoria
6030

Wavemere
Fostoria
6030/3

Buttercup
Fostoria
6030, Etch 340

Christiana
Fostoria
6030, Cut 814

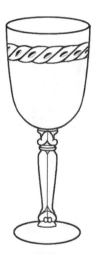

Gadroon
Fostoria
6030, Cut 816

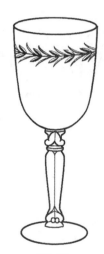

Holly
Fostoria
6030, Cut 815

Trellis
Fostoria
6030, Cut 822

Stem 6031
Fostoria

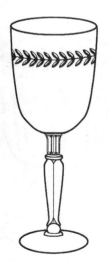

Mount Vernon
Fostoria
6031, Cut 817

Tempo
Fostoria
6032

Formality
Fostoria
6032, Cut 818

Greek Key
Fostoria
6032, Cut 819

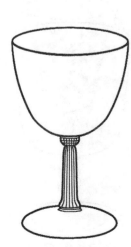

Mademoiselle
Fostoria
6033

Bouquet
Fostoria
6033, Etch 342

Reflection
Fostoria
6033, Platinum Dec. 625

Spinet
Fostoria
6033, Cut 821

Sprite
Fostoria
6033, Cut 823

Rutledge
Fostoria
6036

Ballet
Fostoria
6036, Cut 828

Camellia
Fostoria
6036, Etch 344

Chatham
Fostoria
6036, Cut 829

Rose
Fostoria
6036, Cut 827

Silver Flutes
Fostoria
6037

Heather
Fostoria
6037, Etch 343

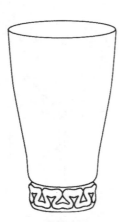

Tiara
Fostoria
6044

Capri
Fostoria
6045

Marquise
Fostoria
6045, Cut 831

Rondo
Fostoria
6045, Cut 830

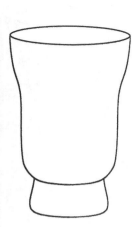

Catalina
Fostoria
6046

Windsor
Fostoria
6049

Avalon
Fostoria
6049, Cut 832

Bridal Wreath
Fostoria
6049, Cut 833

Starflower
Fostoria
6049, Etch 345

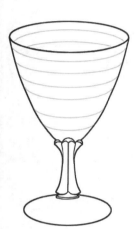

Ringlet
Fostoria
6051, Optic

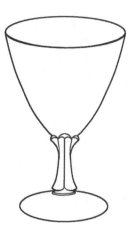

Courtship
Fostoria
6051 ½

Bracelet
Fostoria
6051 ½, Cut 838

Nosegay
Fostoria
6051 ½, Cut 834

Plume
Fostoria
6051 ½, Cut 839

Wedding Ring
Fostoria
6051 ½, Plat. Dec. 626

Wheat
Fostoria
6051 ½, Cut 837

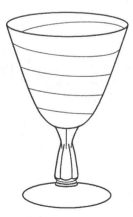

Moon Ring
Fostoria
6052

Continental
Fostoria
6052 ½

Ingrid
Fostoria
6052 ½, Cut 836

Pine
Fostoria
6052 ½, Cut 835

Thistle
Fostoria
6052 ½, Etch 346

Marilyn
Fostoria
6055

Shell Pearl
Fostoria
6055, Iridescent

Rhapsody
Fostoria
6055 ½

Anniversary
Fostoria
6055 ½, Gold Dec. 634

Circlet
Fostoria
6055 ½, Cut 840

Spray
Fostoria
6055 ½, Cut 841

Diadem
Fostoria
6056

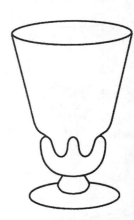

Chalice
Fostoria
6059

Contour
Fostoria
6060

Spring
Fostoria
6060, Cut 844

Sylvan
Fostoria
6060, Crystal Print 1

Windfall
Fostoria
6060, Cut 870

Lyric
Fostoria
6061

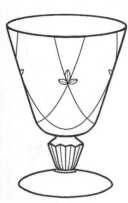

Crest
Fostoria
6061, Cut 843

Regal
Fostoria
6061, Cut 842

Skyflower
Fostoria
6061, Crystal Print 2

Patrician
Fostoria
6064

Maytime
Fostoria
6064, Cut 845

Rosette
Fostoria
6064, Crystal Print 3

Skylark
Fostoria
6064, Cut 846

Elegance
Fostoria
6064 ½

Cascade
Fostoria
6064 ½, Iridescent

Symphony
Fostoria
6065

Ambassador
Fostoria
6065, Gold Dec. 637

Baronet
Fostoria
6065, Cut 847

Heritage
Fostoria
6065, Cut 849

Legacy
Fostoria
6065, Plat. Dec. 635

Living Rose
Fostoria
6065, Crystal Print 5

Lynwood
Fostoria
6065, Crystal Print 4

Swirl
Fostoria
6065, Cut 848

Puritan
Fostoria
6068

April Love
Fostoria
6068, Cut 866

Autumn
Fostoria
6068, Cut 850

Gossamer
Fostoria
6068, Cut 852

Stardust
Fostoria
6068, Cut 851

Victoria
Fostoria
6068 ½

Prelude
Fostoria
6071

Kimberly
Fostoria
6071, Cut 855

Celeste
Fostoria
6072

Bridal Belle
Fostoria
6072, Cut 639, Plat.

Melody
Fostoria
6072, Cut 881

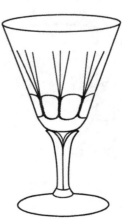

Moonbeam
Fostoria
6072, Cut 856

Enchantment
Fostoria
6074

Golden Love
Fostoria
6074, Dec. 640, Gold Trim

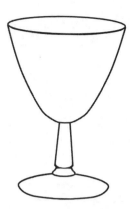

Nordic
Fostoria
6077

American Beauty
Fostoria
6077, Cut 858

Garland
Fostoria
6077, Cut 859

Kent
Fostoria
6079

Empress
Fostoria
6079, Cut 861

Williamsburg
Fostoria
6079, Cut 874

Fascination
Fostoria
6080

Carousel
Fostoria
6080, Cut 863

Classic Gold
Fostoria
6080, Gold Dec. 641

Trousseau
Fostoria
6080, Plat. Dec. 642

True Love
Fostoria
6080, Cut 862

Firelight
Fostoria
6080 ½, Irid. Dec. 657

Embassy
Fostoria
6083

Golden Grail
Fostoria
6083, Gold Dec. 644

Fostoria

St. Regis
Fostoria
6083, Cut 873

Westminster
Fostoria
6083, Cut 872

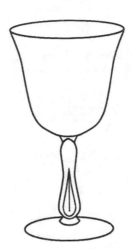

Petite
Fostoria
6085

Golden Lace
Fostoria
6085, Dec. 645, Gold Trim

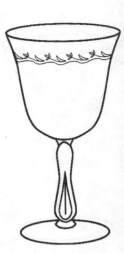

Juliet
Fostoria
6085, Cut 865

Moonglow
Fostoria
6085, Dec. 649, Plat. Trim

Sunglow
Fostoria
6085, Dec. 650, Gold Trim

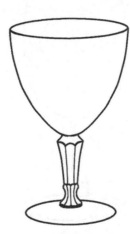

Vesper
Fostoria
6086

Fantasy
Fostoria
6086, Crystal Print 17

Overture
Fostoria
6086, Cut 867

Serenade
Fostoria
6086, Cut 864

Star Song
Fostoria
6086, Cut 871

Chateau
Fostoria
6087

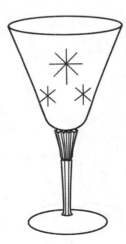

Evening Star
Fostoria
6087, Cut 869

Golden Flair
Fostoria
6087, Gold Dec. 643

Orleans
Fostoria
6089

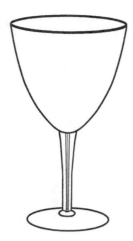

Beloved
Fostoria
6089, Plat. Dec. 647

Bridal Crown
Fostoria
6089, Cut 882

Devon
Fostoria
6089, Cut 876

Whisper
Fostoria
6089, Cut 875

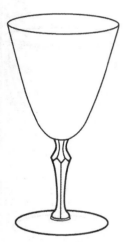

Priscilla
Fostoria
6092

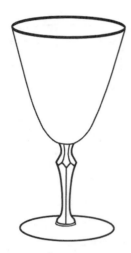

Aurora
Fostoria
6092, Gold Dec. 651

Burgundy
Fostoria
6092, Cut 878

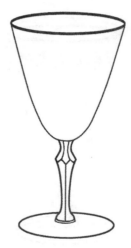

Engagement
Fostoria
6092, Plat. Dec. 648

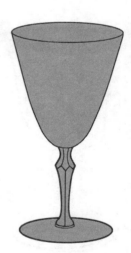

Regal
Fostoria
6092, Stainless Plated

Spring Song
Fostoria
6092, Cut 884

Sweetheart Rose
Fostoria
6092, Cut 877

Twilight
Fostoria
6092, Cut 883

Bristol
Fostoria
6093, Cut 880

Stockholm
Fostoria
6093, Cut 879

Fostoria

Sheraton
Fostoria
6097

Andover
Fostoria
6097, Etch 665, Gold

Georgian
Fostoria
6097, Cut 885

Gloucester
Fostoria
6097, Cut 898

Harvest
Fostoria
6097, Rust Bowl

Richmond
Fostoria
6097, Gold Dec. 654

Sentimental
Fostoria
6097, Crystal Print 25

Sheffield
Fostoria
6097, Plat. Dec. 653

Vogue
Fostoria
6099

Candlelight
Fostoria
6099, Plat. Dec. 652

Chapel Bells
Fostoria
6099, Cut 888

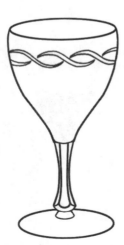

Embrace
Fostoria
6099, Cut 887

Golden Song
Fostoria
6099, Dec. 662, Gold Trim

Love Song
Fostoria
6099, Dec. 655, Plat. Trim

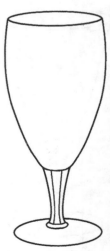

Debutante
Fostoria
6100

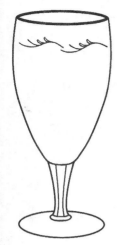

Bridesmaid
Fostoria
6100, Dec. 658, Plat. Trim

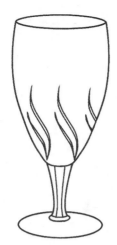

Cotillion
Fostoria
6100, Cut 892

Evening Breeze
Fostoria
6100, Cut 891

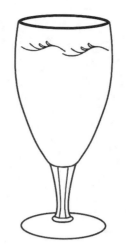

Flower Girl
Fostoria
6100, Dec. 659, Gold Trim

Princess Ann
Fostoria
6100, Cut 893

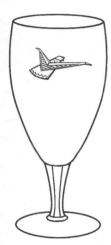

Thunderbird
Fostoria
6100

Crystal Twist
Fostoria
6101

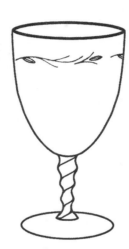

Coronet
Fostoria
6101, Dec. 656, Plat. Trim

Flower Song
Fostoria
6101, Cut 894

Silhouette
Fostoria
6102

Bianca
Fostoria
6102, Crystal Print 22

Bridal Shower
Fostoria
6102, Cut 897

Fleurette
Fostoria
6102, Crystal Print 26

Invitation
Fostoria
6102, Plat. Dec. 660

Milady
Fostoria
6102, Cut 895

Fostoria

Platina Rose
Fostoria
6102, Dec. 663, Plat. Trim

Rosalie
Fostoria
6102, Crystal Print 19

Venus
Fostoria
6102, Cut 896

Vermeil
Fostoria
6102, Gold Dec. 661

Wedding Flower
Fostoria
6102, Cut 920

Glamour
Fostoria
6103

Announcement
Fostoria
6103, Plat. Dec. 666

Ballerina
Fostoria
6103, Cut 900

Barcelona
Fostoria
6103, Etch 27

Cherish
Fostoria
6103, Gray/Plat. Dec. 681

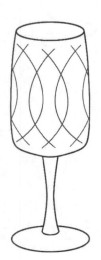

Forever
Fostoria
6103, Cut 90

Nuptial
Fostoria
6103, Etch 21

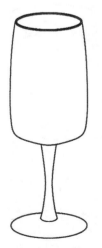

Rehearsal
Fostoria
6103, Gold Dec. 667

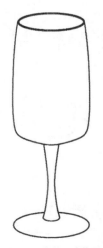

Something Blue
Fostoria
6103, Blue/Plat. Dec. 685

Jefferson
Fostoria
6104

110

Carillon
Fostoria
6104, Cut 915

Monte Carlo
Fostoria
6104, Cut 912

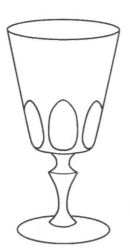

Queen Anne
Fostoria
6104, Cut 905

Savannah
Fostoria
6104, Cut 902

Tiara
Fostoria
6104, Cut 903

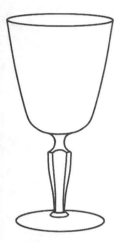

Berkshire
Fostoria
6105

Cantata
Fostoria
6105, Cut 907

Georgetown
Fostoria
6105, Cut 906

Celebrity
Fostoria
6106

Brocade
Fostoria
6106, Gold Dec. 674

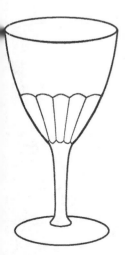

Empire
Fostoria
6106, Cut 908

Mantilla
Fostoria
6106, Plat. Dec. 675

Inspiration
Fostoria
6107

Allegro
Fostoria
6107, Gold Dec. 672

Betrothal
Fostoria
6107, Plat. Dec. 673

Fostoria

Matrimony
Fostoria
6107, Cut 910

Orange Blossom
Fostoria
6107, Cut 911

Remembrance
Fostoria
6107, Gold Dec. 670

Precedence
Fostoria
6108

Exeter
Fostoria
6109

Promise
Fostoria
6110

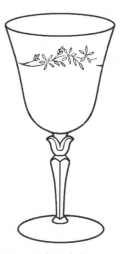

Glendale
Fostoria
6110, Cut 919

Golden Belle
Fostoria
6110, Gold Dec. 677

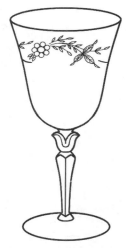

Greenfield
Fostoria
6110, Cut 916

Reception
Fostoria
6110, Platinum Trim

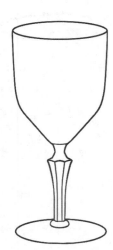

Illusion
Fostoria
6111

First Love
Fostoria
6111, Cut 918

Olympic
Fostoria
6111, Gold or Platinum

Renaissance
Fostoria
6111, Gold or Platinum

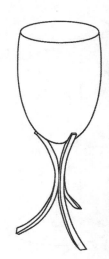

Triumph
Fostoria
6112, Gold or Silver

Moon Mist
Fostoria
6113, Frosted Dec. 684

Versailles
Fostoria
6113, Gold Dec. 683

Venture
Fostoria
6114, Gray Base

Eloquence
Fostoria
6120

Contrast
Fostoria
6120, Black & White

Venise
Fostoria
6120, Dec. 688, Plat. Trim

Sphere
Fostoria
6121

Biscayne
Fostoria
6122

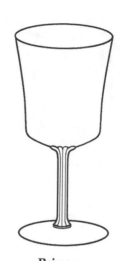

Princess
Fostoria
6123, Clear, Blue, or with Platinum

Cameo
Fostoria
6123, Cry. Print 28, Green

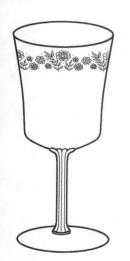

Intimate
Fostoria
123, Cry. Print 31, Blue

Marquis
Fostoria
6123, Dec. 692, Plat. Trim

Petit Fleur
Fostoria
6123, Cut 922

Poetry
Fostoria
6123, Crystal Print 32

Tenderness
Fostoria
6123, Plat. Dec. 691, Green

Fostoria

Splendor
Fostoria
6124

Brocade
Fostoria
6124, Crystal Print 30

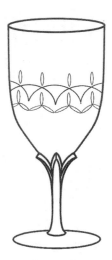

Granada
Fostoria
6124, Cut 923

Distinction
Fostoria
6125

Wimbledon
Fostoria
6126, Clear

Corsage Plum
Fostoria
6126, Purple Stem

Gazebo
Fostoria
6126, Black or Rust Base

Tara
Fostoria
6126, Etch 34

Festive
Fostoria
6127

Serenity
Fostoria
6127

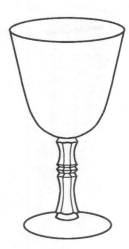

Regency
Fostoria
6128

Heirloom
Fostoria
6128, Etch 36

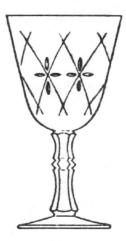

Nova
Fostoria
6128, Cut 934

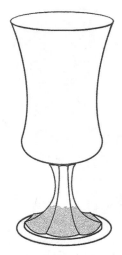

Misty
Fostoria
6129, Various Colors

Pavilion
Fostoria
6143

Nouveau
Fostoria
6143, Etch 42

Lotus
Fostoria
6144

Gala
Fostoria
6147, Crystal

Celebration
Fostoria
6147, Plat. Dec. 698

Festival
Fostoria
6147, Etch 45

Icicle
Fostoria
6147, Frosted Base

Jubilee
Fostoria
6147, Gold Dec. 699

Maypole
Fostoria
6149, Various Colors

Athens
Fostoria
AT01, Romania

Atlanta
Fostoria
Cut, Romania

Aura
Fostoria
AV02, Romania

Baroness
Fostoria
Cut, Romania

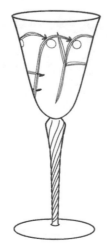

Bellwether
Fostoria
BE05, Romania

Bennington
Fostoria
BE04

Captiva
Fostoria
CA18, Machine Made

Carmel
Fostoria
Gray Cut, Romania

Charleston
Fostoria
Cut, Romania

Chippendale
Fostoria
CH05

Countess
Fostoria
Cut, Romania

Engagement
Fostoria
Gold Trim

Jolie
Fostoria
Clear, Romania

Juniper
Fostoria
JU05

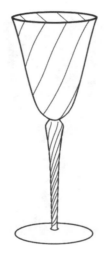

Liana
Fostoria, Romania
Gold or Platinum Trim

Monet
Fostoria
MO12

Northampton
Fostoria
N006

San Francisco
Fostoria
Cut, Romania

Satin Ribbons
Fostoria
SA05

Stephanie
Fostoria
Cut, Romania

Brilliant
Fostoria
Line 1001, Tableware

Coventry
Fostoria
Cut 807, Tableware

Gold Lace
Fostoria
Decoration 514

Heirloom
Fostoria
Decorative Ware

Lacy Leaf
Fostoria
Crystal Print 6

Milkweed
Fostoria
Crystal Print 7

Morning Glory
Fostoria
Carving 12, Giftware

Rosby
Fostoria
Line 1704

Seascape
Fostoria
Line 2685, Opalescent

Bacchus
France
"God of Wine"

Argenta
Franconia
Platinum Trim

Arietta
Franconia

Athene
Franconia
Gold Trim

Classic
Franconia

Continental
Franconia

Delphine
Franconia

Fascination
Franconia

Harmony
Franconia

Hawthorn
Franconia

Irina
Franconia

Jewel
Franconia
Gold Trim

Karat
Franconia

Laurel Oak
Franconia

Regal
Franconia

Regent
Franconia

Silver Thistle
Franconia

Stella
Franconia

Aran
Galway
Newer

Baldmore
Galway

Burren Suite
Galway

Cashel
Galway

Rathmore
Galway

Spindrift
Galway

GAL 1
Galway

Blarney
Galway

Claddaugh
Galway
Cut and Etched

Keenan
Galway

King's Court
Galway

Shannon
Galway

Carrick
Galway

Erin
Galway

Leah
Galway
Laurel & Hatch

Longford
Galway

Aran
Galway
Older

Ashford
Galway

Castlerosse
Galway

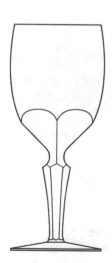

Oyster
Galway

119

Corrib
Galway

Killarney
Galway

Old Galway
Galway
Cut or Plain Base

Royal Irish
Galway
Cut or Plain Base

Claddaugh
Galway
Older

Clifden
Galway

Connemara
Galway

O'Brien
Galway
Cut or Plain Base

O'Donnell
Galway

Camelot
Galway

Claddaugh Ring
Galway

Harvest
Galway

Kaitlyn
Galway

Michaun
Galway

Terese
Galway

Coleraine
Galway

Leah
Galway
Laurel & Thumbprint

Patricia
Galway

Deirdre
Galway

O'Hara
Galway

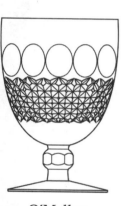

O'Malley
Galway

Ardmore
Galway

21-1
Glastonbury/Lotus
Etched, Gold Bands (pink)

37-1
Glastonbury/Lotus
Gray Wheat

37-2
Glastonbury/Lotus
Gold Wheat and Trim

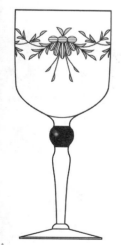

37-3
Glastonbury/Lotus
Ruby Ball

54-1
Glastonbury/Lotus

54-2
Glastonbury/Lotus

67-1
Glastonbury/Lotus

67-2
Glastonbury/Lotus

67-3
Glastonbury/Lotus

75-1
Glastonbury/Lotus
Gold Bands

77-3
Glastonbury/Lotus
Platinum Bands

78-1
Glastonbury/Lotus

78-2
Glastonbury/Lotus
Platinum Bands

80-1
Glastonbury/Lotus
Gold Encrusted

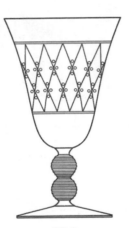

80-2
Glastonbury/Lotus

81-1
Glastonbury/Lotus
Gold

85-1
Glastonbury/Lotus
Gold Encrusted

89-1
Glastonbury/Lotus

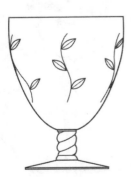

94-1
Glastonbury/Lotus
Vine

97-2
Glastonbury/Lotus

98-2
Glastonbury/Lotus
Cut Rose

470-1
Glastonbury/Lotus
Gold Encrusted

553-1
Glastonbury/Lotus
Cut, Gold

553-2
Glastonbury/Lotus
Platinum

896-1
Glastonbury/Lotus
Cut Rose

965-2
Glastonbury/Lotus

969-1
Glastonbury/Lotus
Gray Wheat

984-1
Glastonbury/Lotus

1500-1
Glastonbury/Lotus

1500-2
Glastonbury/Lotus

2008-1
Glastonbury/Lotus
Platinum Band and Foot

3720-1
Glastonbury/Lotus

Belmont Leaf
Glastonbury/Lotus
10, Gray Cutting

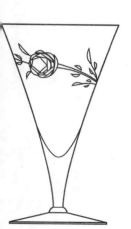

Contemporary Rose
Glastonbury/Lotus
L13

Hostess
Glastonbury/Lotus
3411

Laurelwood
Glastonbury/Lotus
L31, Gold Encrusted

Majesty
Glastonbury/Lotus
78, Cut 24

Monterey
Glastonbury/Lotus
3720

Puritan
Glastonbury/Lotus
87, Platinum

GO 1
Goebel

Cavalier
Gorham
1493, Wide Platinum

Elegance
Gorham
1493, Clear and Colored

First Lady
Gorham
1493, Narrow Plat. Trim

Grandee
Gorham
1493, Wide Gold Trim

Marquis
Gorham
1493

Prelude
Gorham
1493, Smoke, Plat. Trim

President
Gorham
1493, Narrow Gold Trim

Valencia
Gorham
1493, Brown, Gold Trim

Viscount
Gorham
1493, Older

Accent
Gorham
aka "Accent II"

Images
Gorham
Various Colors

Autumn
Gorham
Brown Bowl, Gold Trim

Firelight
Gorham
1548, Gold Trim

Lark
Gorham
1548

Midnight Mist
Gorham
1548, Gray Bowl, Plat. Trim

Moonrise
Gorham
1548, aka "Moonglow"

Rosemist
Gorham
1548, Pink Bowl

Spring
Gorham
1548, Green, also
with Platinum

Summer Sky
Gorham
1548, Blue, also
with Platinum

Twilight
Gorham
1548, Gray

Gigi
Gorham
6447

Fidelity
Gorham (Alvin)
Undecorated

Aura
Gorham
Gold Trim

Platina
Gorham
6036, Platinum Trim

Candlelight
Gorham
1463, Platinum Trim

Enchantment
Gorham
1463, Gold Trim

Francine
Gorham
1463, Pink Bowl

Gourmet
Gorham
1463

Cabachon Ruby
Gorham
9024, Red Bowl

"21" Club
Gorham, Red Wine
Wine Tasting Series

Tempo
Gorham
206

Platinum Smoke
Gorham
6027, Gray Base, Plat. Trim

Adrian
Gorham
6009, Cut, Gold Trim

Chanson
Gorham
6009, Cut, Platinum Trim

Fontana
Gorham
6009

Mansfield
Gorham
6009, Gold Trim

Montclair
Gorham
6009, Platinum Trim

Blue Smoke
Gorham
6010, Blue/Gray Bowl

Evensong
Gorham
6010, Smoke, Platinum Trim

Rubiat
Gorham
6010, Ruby Bowl

Chateau Rose
Gorham

Rondelle
Gorham
Platinum Trim

Triomphe
Gorham
Gold Design

Arabesque
Gorham

Joelle
Gorham

Provender
Gorham
Gold Trim

Revenna
Gorham

Regina
Gorham

Lotus
Gorham

Primrose
Gorham

Diamond
Gorham
Also with Gold Trim

Borealis
Gorham
Gray Cut

Gabrielle
Gorham

Star Blossom
Gorham
Plain or with Gold Trim

Trinity
Gorham

Eilish
Gorham

Bellevue
Gorham

Lady Spencer
Gorham

Sundance
Gorham
Plain or with Gold Trim

Bellamy
Gorham
Gold or Platinum Trim

Romantique
Gorham
Plain or with Gold Trim

Acacia
Gorham
Frosted Cutting

Laurin
Gorham
Also with Gold or Plat.

Castlefield
Gorham
Cut

Patrician
Gorham
Gold Trim

Theme Gold
Gorham
Also "Theme Platinum"

Chantilly
Gorham

Hearthglow
Gorham

Fairfax
Gorham

Hispana
Gorham
1637

Viscount
Gorham
Newer

Sheffield
Gorham
7044, made by Barthmann

Diamond
Gorham
Hexagonal Base

Stratford
Gorham
1636

Perspective
Gorham
Hexagonal Base

Cathedral
Gorham
Cut, Lightweight

French Cathedral
Gorham
Heavy, Lead Crystal

Grand Baroque
Gorham
1600, Gold Encrusted

Royal Tivoli
Gorham
Heavy, Lead Crystal

Tivoli
Gorham
1608, Lightweight

Royal Vienna
Gorham
1660

Baronial
Gorham

Ariana
Gorham
Cut

Southampton
Gorham

Embassy
Gorham
1111

Monticello
Gorham
1110

Pristine
Gorham
1112

de Medici
Gorham

Accolade
Gorham

Melrose
Gorham

Rosewood
Gorham

Alexandra
Gorham

Norfolk
Gorham

Althea
Gorham

Aspen
Gorham

Crown Point
Gorham

La Scala
Gorham

Strasbourg
Gorham

Barronscourt
Gorham

King Arthur
Gorham

Accolade Gold
Gorham
Cut, Gold Trim

Rosecliff
Gorham

Royal Devon
Gorham
Gold Trim

Clermont
Gorham, Various Colors
Also with Gold Trim

Bellingham
Gorham

Golden Sunset
Gorham
Gold Trim

Sunset
Gorham

Glenwood
Gorham

Golden Glenwood
Gorham
Gold Trim

Lady Anne
Gorham

Lady Anne Gold
Gorham
Gold Trim

Nocturne
Gorham

Florentine
Gorham

King Charles
Gorham
Newer, Faceted Stem

Lady Madison
Gorham

Raphael
Gorham

Chancellor
Gorham

Esprit
Gorham

Glen Mist
Gorham

King Edward
Gorham

Stanford
Gorham

Winfield
Gorham

Bamberg
Gorham

Anthem
Gorham

Cherrywood
Gorham
Also with Gold Trim and Ruby

Renaissance
Gorham
9024, made by Barthmann

Westminster
Gorham
9039, made by Barthmann

Marlborough
Gorham
9060, made by Barthmann

Richelieu
Gorham
7062, aka "Rondo"

Citadel
Gorham
aka "Epic"

Fidelio
Gorham
Notched Stem

Sonja
Gorham

GOR 1
Gorham

Juliana
Gorham

Lady Slipper
Gorham

Maxine
Gorham

Queen's Way
Gorham

Serena
Gorham

Snow Blossom
Gorham

Pastelle
Gorham
Orchid Color

St. Pierre
Gorham
Blue Stem and Base

Stardust
Gorham
Peach Color

Vie en Rose
Gorham
Pink

Andante
Gorham
Plain or with Gold Trim

Celeste
Gorham
Cut, Platinum Trim

Jolie
Gorham

Christina
Gorham
Light, Blown

Golden Horizon
Gorham
Gold Trim

Augusta
Gorham
Optic

Kira
Gorham

Joy
Gorham
Gold Accent

Bridal Bouquet
Gorham
Platinum Trim

Gorham Gold
Gorham
Gold Trim

Gorham Platinum
Gorham
Platinum Trim

Kingsbury
Gorham
Platinum Trim

Monet
Gorham
Platinum Trim

Renoir
Gorham
1659

Minstrel
Gorham
Colored, Gold/Platinum Ba

Octette
Gorham
Various Colors

Rosefire
Gorham
Pink

Golden Rondelle
Gorham
Frosted Ball, Gold Accent

Newport
Gorham

Classique Gold
Gorham
Gold Trim

Alyssum
Gorham
Frosted Stem

Chapelle
Gorham

Excelsior
Gorham

Isabella
Gorham

King Charles
Gorham
Older, Short Stem

Crystalline
Gorham
Various Colors

Decor
Gorham
Various Colors

Fanfare
Gorham
Various Colors

Gentry
Gorham
Various Colors

Chiquita
Gorham
Various Colors

Zest
Gorham
Various Colors

Carrington
Gorham
Barware

Monte Carlo
Gorham
Barware

Olive Cut
Gorham
Barware

Spring Meadows
Gorham
Barware

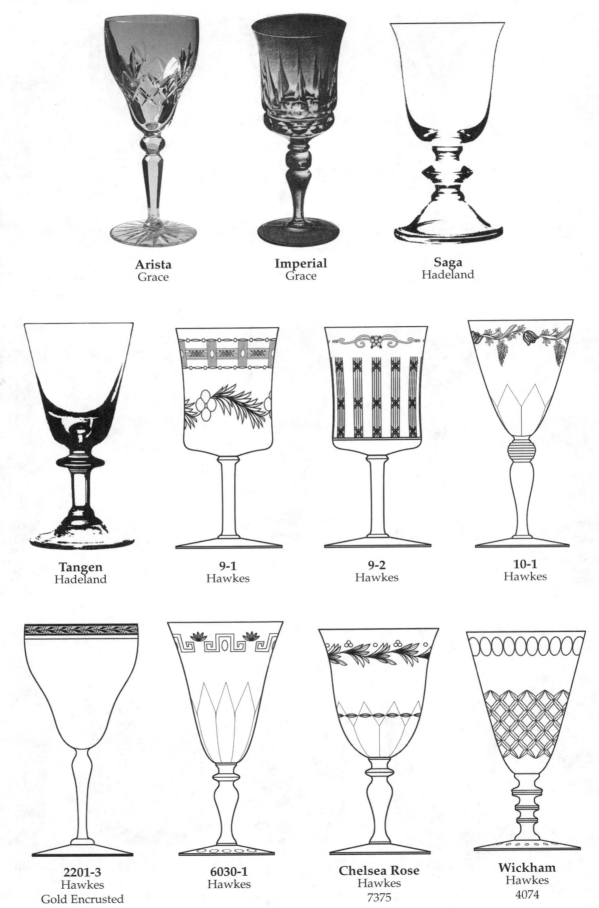

Arista
Grace

Imperial
Grace

Saga
Hadeland

Tangen
Hadeland

9-1
Hawkes

9-2
Hawkes

10-1
Hawkes

2201-3
Hawkes
Gold Encrusted

6030-1
Hawkes

Chelsea Rose
Hawkes
7375

Wickham
Hawkes
4074

1E92	150	300	325	341	347	348	351	352
Page 139	*Page 139*	*Page 139*	*Page 139*	*Page 139*	*Page 139*	*Page 139*	*Page 139*	*Page 139*
357	359	373	393	407	411	419	433	451
Page 139	*Page 139*	*Page 139*	*Page 139*	*Page 140*	*Page 140*	*Page 140*	*Page 140*	*Page 140*
1118	1170	1184	1201	1205	1235	1252	1255	1401
Page 140	*Page 140*	*Page 140*	*Page 140*	*Page 140*	*Page 140*	*Page 140*	*Page 140*	*Page 140*
1404	1405	1423	1425	1469	1483	1485	1506	1540
Page 140	*Page 141*	*Page 141*	*Page 141*	*Page 141*	*Page 141*	*Page 141*	*Page 141*	*Page 141*
1567	1776	3308	3312	3317	3320	3324	3333	3335
Page 141	*Page 141*	*Page 141*	*Page 141*	*Page 141*	*Page 141*	*Page 142*	*Page 142*	*Page 142*
3350	3355	3357	3360	3362	3366	3368	3370	3373
Page 142	*Page 142*	*Page 142*	*Page 142*	*Page 143*	*Page 143*	*Page 143*	*Page 143*	*Page 143*

Heisey Shapes and Lines

| 3380 Page 143 | 3381 Page 143 | 3389 Page 144 | 3390 Page 144 | 3404 Page 144 | 3408 Page 145 | 3411 Page 145 | 3414 Page 146 | 3416 Page 146 |

| 3418 Page 146 | 3424 Page 146 | 4002 Page 146 | 4044 Page 146 | 4054 Page 147 | 4055 Page 147 | 4069 Page 147 | 4085 Page 147 | 4090 Page 147 |

| 4091 Page 148 | 4092 Page 148 | 5003 Page 148 | 5009 Page 148 | 5010 Page 148 | 5013 Page 149 | 5019 Page 149 | 5022 Page 149 | 5023 Page 149 |

| 5024 Page 149 | 5025 Page 149 | 5040 Page 150 | 5041 Page 150 | 5057 Page 150 | 5067 Page 150 | 5072 Page 150 | 5074 Page 150 | 5077 Page 150 |

| 5082 Page 150 | 5086 Page 151 | 5089 Page 151 | 5098 Page 151 | 6003 Page 151 | 6004 Page 151 | 6010 Page 151 | 6060 Page 151 | 6091 Page 152 |

Other lines and patterns — page 152.

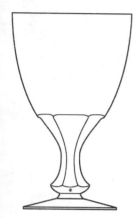

Omega
Heisey
1E92

Melody
Heisey
1E92, Cut 1092

Wheat
Heisey
1E92, Cut 1091

Banded Flute
Heisey
150

Colonial
Heisey
300

Pillows
Heisey
325

Puritan
Heisey
341

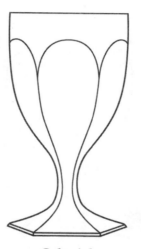

Colonial
Heisey
347

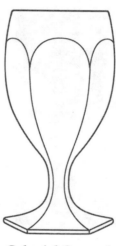

Colonial Cupped
Heisey
348

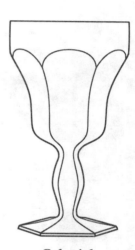

Colonial
Heisey
351

Flat Panel
Heisey
352

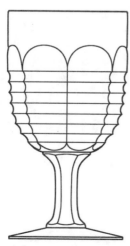

Prison Stripes
Heisey
357

Colonial
Heisey
359

Colonial
Heisey
373

Narrow Flute
Heisey
393

Coarse Rib
Heisey
407

Rib & Panel
Heisey
411

Sussex
Heisey
419

Greek Key
Heisey
433

Cross Lined Flute
Heisey
451

Indian Hill
Heisey
1118, Grapefruit

Pleat & Panel
Heisey
1170

Yeoman
Heisey
1184

Fandango
Heisey
1201

Fancy Loop
Heisey
1205

Beaded Sunburst
Heisey
1235

Twist
Heisey
1252

Pineapple & Fan
Heisey
1255

Empress
Heisey
1401

Old Sandwich
Heisey
1404

Ipswich
Heisey
1405, Square Base

Sweet Ad-O-Line
Heisey
1423

Victorian
Heisey
1425

Ridgeleigh
Heisey
1469, Heavy Pressed

Stanhope
Heisey
1483

Saturn
Heisey
1485

Whirlpool
Heisey
1506

Lariat
Heisey
1540, Heavy Pressed

Moonglo
Heisey
1540, Cut 980

Plantation
Heisey
1567, Heavy Pressed

Kalonyal
Heisey
1776

Peacock
Heisey
3308, Etch 366

Monticello
Heisey
3312, Etch 163

Tatting
Heisey
3317, Etch 33

Trellis
Heisey
3320, Cut 697

Delaware
Heisey
3324

Old Glory
Heisey
3333

Renaissance
Heisey
3333, Etch 413

Trefoil
Heisey
3333

Victory
Heisey
3335, Etch 431

Wabash
Heisey
3350

Frontenac
Heisey
3350, Etch 440

Mayflower
Heisey
3350, Etch 166

Pied Piper
Heisey
3350, Etch 439

Fairacre
Heisey
3355

3355-1
Heisey

King Arthur
Heisey
3357

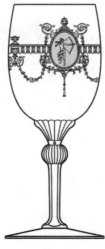

Diana
Heisey
3357, Etch 442

Penn Charter
Heisey
3360

Olympiad
Heisey
3360, Etch 458

St. Anne
Heisey
3360, Cut 781

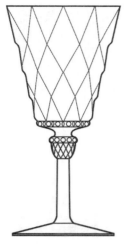

Charter Oak
Heisey
3362

Trojan
Heisey
3366

Trojan
Heisey
3366, Etch 445

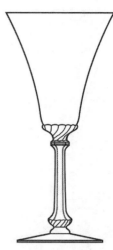

Albemarle
Heisey
3368

Champlain
Heisey
3368, Cut 909

Chateau
Heisey
3368, Cut 867

Trojan
Heisey
3368, Etch 445

African
Heisey
3370

Morning Glory
Heisey
3373

Old Dominion
Heisey
3380

Empress
Heisey
3380, Etch 447

Old Colony
Heisey
3380, Etch 448

Titania
Heisey
3380, Etch 456

Creole
Heisey
3381

Duquesne
Heisey
3389

Botticelli
Heisey
3389, Cut 848

Chintz
Heisey
3389, Etch 450

Continental
Heisey
3389, Cut 832

Everglade
Heisey
3389, Cut 913

Normandie
Heisey
3389, Etch 480

Carcassone
Heisey
3390

Formal Chintz
Heisey
3390, Etch 450 ½

Lafayette
Heisey
3390, Etch 451

Old Colony
Heisey
3390, Etch 448

Spanish
Heisey
3404

Aberdeen
Heisey
3404, Cut 789

Barcelona
Heisey
3404, Cut 941

Florentine
Heisey
3404, Cut 865

Killarney
Heisey
3404, Cut 797

Monterey
Heisey
3404, Cut 793

Riviere
Heisey
3404, Cut 794

Streamline
Heisey
3404, Cut 847

Titania
Heisey
3404, Etch 456

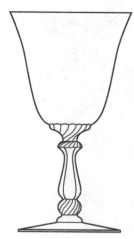

Jamestown
Heisey
3408

Barcelona
Heisey
3408, Cut 941

Candlelight
Heisey
3408

Kent
Heisey
3408, Cut 866

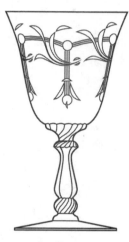

Larkspur
Heisey
3408, Cut 835

Narcissus
Heisey
3408, Cut 965

Palmetto
Heisey
3408, Cut 816

Rosalie
Heisey
3408, Etch 497

Sheffield
Heisey
3408, Cut 985

Sweet Briar
Heisey
3408, Cut 812

Monte Cristo
Heisey
3411

Kalarama
Heisey
3411, Cut 851

Manchester
Heisey
3411, Cut 802

Olympiad
Heisey
3411, Etch 458

Roxy
Heisey
3411, Cut 829

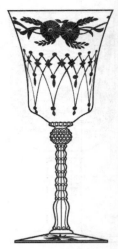

Waikiki
Heisey
3411, Cut 801

Titania
Heisey
3414, Etch 456

Barbara Fritchie
Heisey
3416

Delmonte
Heisey
3416, Cut 850

Manhattan
Heisey
3416, Cut 799

Titania
Heisey
3416, Etch 456

Will o' the Wisp
Heisey
3416, Cut 795

Neo Classic
Heisey, Square Base
3418, Cut 846

Admiralty
Heisey
3424, Square Base

Calcutta
Heisey
4002, Cut 809

New Era
Heisey
4044

Sea Glade
Heisey
4044, Cut 825

Venus
Heisey
4044, Cut 826

Coronation
Heisey
4054

Park Lane
Heisey
4055

Briar Cliff
Heisey
4055, Cut 840

Nomad
Heisey
4055, Cut 849

Piccadilly
Heisey
4055, Cut 844

Singapore
Heisey
4055, Cut 842

Ridgeleigh
Heisey
4069, Thin Blown

Mariemont
Heisey
4069, Cut 872

Sylvia
Heisey
4069, Cut 875

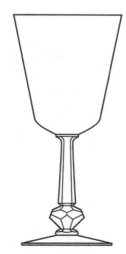

Kohinoor
Heisey
4085

Berkeley Square
Heisey
4085, Cut 892

Pembroke
Heisey
4085, Cut 891

Zeuse
Heisey
4090, Cut 903

Kimberly
Heisey
4091

Belfast
Heisey
4091, Cut 943

Courtship
Heisey
4091, Cut 944

Dolly Madison Rose
Heisey
4091, Cut 1015

Laurel Wreath
Heisey
4091, Cut 919

Sungate
Heisey
4091, Cut 896

Kenilworth
Heisey
4092

Rosalie
Heisey, Wine
4092, Etch 497

Crystolite
Heisey
5003

Belle Le Rose
Heisey
5009, Etch 501

Everglade
Heisey
5009, Cut 913

Symphone
Heisey
5010

Crinoline
Heisey
5010, Etch 502

Danish Princess
Heisey
5010, Cut 921

Minuet
Heisey
5010, Etch 503

Daisy
Heisey
5013, Cut 924

Waverly
Heisey
5019

Burgundy
Heisey
5019, Cut 1020

Graceful
Heisey
5022

Enchantress
Heisey
5022, Cut 947

Harvester
Heisey
5022, Cut 942

Orchid
Heisey
5022, Etch 507

Continental
Heisey
5023

Evelyn
Heisey
5023, Cut 949

Festoon Wreath
Heisey
5023, Cut 939

Westchester
Heisey
5023, Cut 940

Oxford
Heisey
5024

Inspiration
Heisey
5024, Cut 1074

Maryland
Heisey, Wine
5024, Cut 964

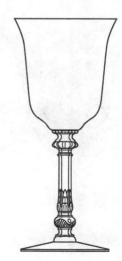

Tyrolean
Heisey
5025

Harvester
Heisey
5025, Cut 942

Orchid
Heisey
5025, Etch 507

Lariat
Heisey
5040, Thin Blown

Moonglo
Heisey
5040, Cut 980

Athena
Heisey
5041

Laurel
Heisey
5057, Cut 1044

Midwest
Heisey
5057, Cut 1059 ½

Peachtree
Heisey
5057, Cut 1017

Plantation
Heisey
5067, Thin Blown

Plantation Ivy
Heisey
5067, Etch 516

Heisey Rose
Heisey
5072, Etch 515

Sea Horse
Heisey
5074

Arcadia
Heisey
5077, Cut 1025

Rosebud
Heisey
5077, Cut 1082

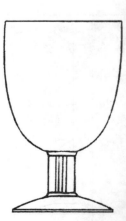

Mid Century
Heisey
5082

Maytime
Heisey
5082, Cut 1034

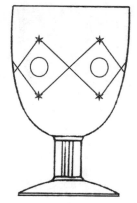

Skyline
Heisey
5082, Cut 1050

Plantation Ivy
Heisey
5086, Etch 516

Nonchalance
Heisey
5089, Cut 1076

Bel Air
Heisey
5098, Cut 1070

Tempo
Heisey
6003

6003-1
Heisey

Garland
Heisey
6003, Cut 1079

Wedding Band
Heisey
6003, Cut 1081

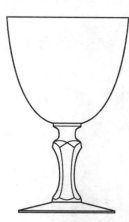

Classic
Heisey
6004

American Beauty
Heisey
6004, Cut 1086

Forget Me Not
Heisey
6004, Cut 1085

Spring
Heisey
6004, Cut 1084

Finesse
Heisey
6010

Greenbrier
Heisey
6060, Cut 1031

Iris
Heisey
6060, Cut 1040

Cabochon
Heisey
6091

Debutante
Heisey
6091, Cut 1066

Holly Hock
Heisey
6091, Cut 1051

Southwind
Heisey
6091, Cut 1072

Starlight
Heisey
6091, Cut 1060

Pinwheel & Fan
Heisey
Line 350

**Prince of Whales,
Plumes**
Heisey, Line 335

**Punty & Diamond
Point**
Heisey, Line 305

Sunflower
Heisey
Line 7000

Foxchase
Heisey
Deep Plate Etch 462

Tally Ho
Heisey
Deep Plate Etch 467

Iris
Hjortur Nielsen

The Byrdes Collection
Hofbauer

HOL 1
Holmegaard
Smoke

Almue
Holmegaard

Atlantic
Holmegaard
Blue/Gray Bowl

Bluebells
Holmegaard

Charlotte Amalie
Holmegaard

Copenhagen
Holmegaard

Danish Hunter
Holmegaard

Danish Ships
Holmegaard

Danish Ships
Holmegaard
Engraved Design

Elsinore
Holmegaard

Ideelle
Holmegaard

Lace
Holmegaard

Largo
Holmegaard

President
Holmegaard

Prince
Holmegaard
Cut Base

Princess
Holmegaard

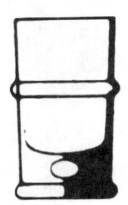

Regiment
Holmegaard
Ice Blue

Scanada
Holmegaard

Tivoli Copenhagen
Holmegaard

Venus
Holmegaard

Wellington
Holmegaard
Cut Stem

Rhododendron
Home Arts

Candlewood
Hoya

Corolle
Hoya

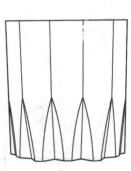

Gothic Spires
Hoya

Horizon
Hoya

Oakwood
Hoya

Sails
Hoya

Sandlewood
Hoya

Teakwood
Hoya

Tulipwood
Hoya

HUC 1
Hunt
Wine

Colchester
Hutschenreuther

Comtesse
Hutschenreuther

Dogwood
Hutschenreuther

Helena
Hutschenreuther

Jasmine
Hutschenreuther

Laurelwood
Hutschenreuther

Suleika
Hutschenreuther

ICH 1
Ichendorf

Aarne
Iittala
2020

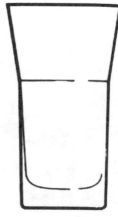

Alvar Aalto
Iittala
2043

Arkipelago
Iittala
2143

Aslak
Iittala
2025

Fiore
Iittala
2116

Gaissa
Iittala
2022

Geo
Iittala
2050

Joiku
Iittala
2107

Kaleva
Iittala
2004

Kalinka
Iittala
2106

Kekkerit
Iittala
Rippled

Kuusi
Iittala
2046

Loimu
Iittala

Marcel
Iittala
2170, Frosted Foot

Marski
Iittala

Metro
Iittala

Nana
Iittala, Opal-White in Glass
2115, also made All Clear

Niva
Iittala
2031

Otso
Iittala
2019

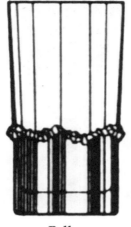

Pallas
Iittala

Ripple
Iittala

Romantica
Iittala

Senator
Iittala
Rippled

Tapio
Iittala
2101, Bubble Stem

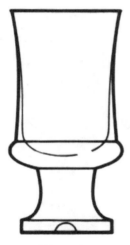

Tavastia
Iittala
2109

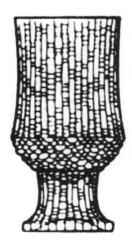

Ultima Thule
Iittala
2132

Alexandra
Imperial Crystals (Imperlux)
363

Astrid
Imperial Crystals (Imperlux)
323

Edinburgh
Imperial Crystals (Imperlux)
103

Rosemary
Imperial Crystals (Imperlux)
308

Windsor
Imperial Crystals (Imperlux)
357

Worcester
Imperial Crystals (Imperlux)
321

Candlewick
Imperial Glass
3400

Dubarry
Imperial Glass
3400, Cut 802

Floral
Imperial Glass
3400, Cut 279

Princess
Imperial Glass
3400, Cut 803

Starlight
Imperial Glass
3400, Cut 108

Valley Lily
Imperial Glass
3400, Cut 800

Wild Rose
Imperial Glass

3400-1
Imperial Glass

3400-2
Imperial Glass

Candlewick
Imperial Glass
400/190

Candlewick
Imperial Glass
400/19

Candlewick
Imperial Glass
4000

Stem 440
Imperial Glass
Gold or Platinum Bands

Simplicity
Imperial Glass
Stem 440

Valencia
Imperial Glass
440, Cut 954

Twist
Imperial Glass
Plain or with Gold or Platinu

Cape Cod
Imperial Glass
1600

Cape Cod
Imperial Glass
1602

Cape Cod
Imperial Glass
3600

Celeste
Imperial Glass
3600, Cut 951

Meander
Imperial Glass
3600, Cut 950

Sophisticate
Imperial Glass
3600, Cut 953

Today
Imperial Glass
3600, Cut 952

China Rose
Imperial Glass
220, Cut 903

Greek Key
Imperial Glass
220, Cut 904

Sunup
Imperial Glass
220/C907

Trousseau
Imperial Glass
210, Cut 814

Winter Berry
Imperial Glass
210, Cut 812

Elegance
Imperial Glass
212, C822

Nobility
Imperial Glass
212, Cut 831

Garden Arbor
Imperial Glass
470

Heritage
Imperial Glass
3750, Gold Trim

Etiquette
Imperial Glass
554

Skanda
Imperial Glass
530, Various Colors

Essex
Imperial Glass
Various Colors

Flower Fair
Imperial Glass
Various Colors

Hoffman House
Imperial Glass
Various Colors

Chroma
Imperial Glass
123, Various Colors

Daisy and Button
Imperial Glass
505, "Turn o' the Century"

Mogul Variant
Imperial Glass
612, "Turn o' the Century"

Old Williamsburg
Imperial Glass
Various Colors

Tradition
Imperial Glass
165

Vintage Grape
Imperial Glass
Various Colors

Zodiac
Imperial Glass
1590, Various Colors

Oxford
Imperial Glass
5024

Provincial
Imperial Glass
Various Colors

Scroll
Imperial Glass
Various Colors

Blossom
Imperial Glass

Continental
Imperial Glass
Various Colors

Dawn
Imperial Glass
3300, Various Colors

Expression
Imperial Glass
Various Colors

Pinch
Imperial Glass
ious Colors, Russel Wright

Exeter
Imperial Glass

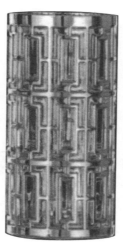

Golden Shoji
Imperial Glass

Spanish Windows
Imperial Glass
Gold Decoration 124

Reflection
Imperial Glass
Various Colors

Svelte
Imperial Glass
330, Various Colors

Bistro
Import Associates

Cascade
Import Associates
Etched

Claudia
Import Associates

Palace
Import Associates

Platinum Band
Import Associates

Silver Lace
Import Associates
Platinum Trim

Victoria
Import Associates
Pink Roses

Octagonal
Independence
Various Colors

Diamond Point
Indiana Glass

Pebble Leaf
Indiana Glass

Recollection
Indiana Glass
Various Colors

Blue Ribbon
Ivima

Clipper Collection
Javit
Safety Lip

Corntime
Javit
150

Fine Wheat
Javit
160

Fragrance
Javit
Safety Lip

Picket
Javit
100

Rain
Javit

Rose
Javit
100

Rose
Javit
160

Rose Collection
Javit
Safety Lip

Seasons
Javit

Sonata
Javit
160, Platinum Trim

Starflower
Javit

Young Love
Javit
160, Platinum Bands

Young Love
Javit
Safety Lip, Platinum Bands

Katherine
J. Jenkins & Sons

JEC 1
Svend Jensen

JEC 2
Svend Jensen

Count
Svend Jensen

Empress
Svend Jensen

Inga
Svend Jensen

Prince
Svend Jensen

Princess
Svend Jensen

163

Queen
Svend Jensen

Spring
Svend Jensen

Stac
Svend Jensen

Tundra
Svend Jensen

Sweetheart Rose
Johann Haviland
Platinum Trim

Wedding Ring
Johann Haviland
Platinum Trim

JOS 1
Josair

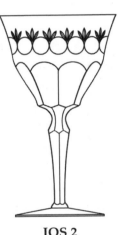

JOS 2
Josair

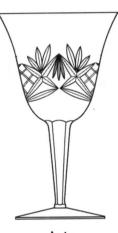

Asta
Josair

Bianca
Josair

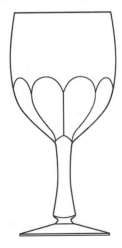

Blanka
Josair

Bonaparte
Josair

Candice
Josair

Colette
Josair

Crest
Josair

Diana
Josair

Dorette
Josair

Dr. Gretsch
Josair

Edith
Josair

Electra
Josair

Emperor
Josair

Empire
Josair

Flare
Josair

Frosted Jasmin
Josair
Frosted Stem

Grace
Josair

Grail
Josair

Independence
Josair

Jacqueline
Josair

Jasmin
Josair

Jutta
Josair

Kaiserin Gold
Josair

Kimberly
Josair

Lynette
Josair

Maria
Josair

Marquise
Josair

Melanie
Josair

Monte Claire
Josair

Montpelier
Josair

Napoleon
Josair

Orleans
Josair

Parma
Josair

Patrician
Josair

Pia
Josair

President
Josair

Pyramid
Josair

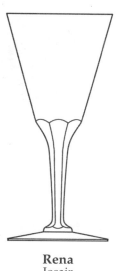

Rena
Josair

Romana
Josair

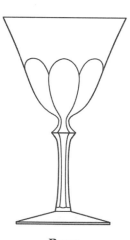

Roxy
Josair

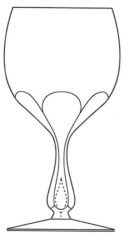

Silhouette
Josair
aka "Etienne"

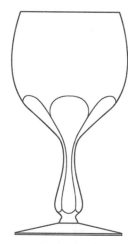

Silhouette
Josair
No Bubble in Stem

Spike Cut
Josair

Symphony
Josair

Tanja
Josair

Theresia
Josair

Ulla
Josair

Versailles
Josair

Viscount
Josair

Vogue
Josair

Louisa
Karhula

Nouveau
Kosta/Boda

Kosta/Boda

Ulrica
Kosta/Boda

Louise
Kosta/Boda

Colombine
Kosta/Boda

Line
Kosta/Boda
Various Color Lines

May
Kosta/Boda

Chateau
Kosta/Boda
Optic

Marie
Kosta/Boda

Ritz
Kosta/Boda

Oktav
Kosta/Boda

Julie
Kosta/Boda

King Karl
Kosta/Boda
Clear or Blue

York I
Kosta/Boda
Smoke

Carmen
Kosta/Boda

Charm
Kosta/Boda

Karlso
Kosta/Boda

Bouquet
Kosta/Boda
8 Point Star

Ann
Kosta/Boda

Rosita
Kosta/Boda

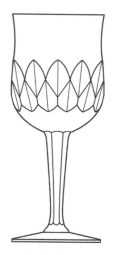

Carl-Gustaf
Kosta/Boda

Alma
Kosta/Boda

Hessler
Kosta/Boda

Helga
Kosta/Boda

Astrid
Kosta/Boda

Rut
Kosta/Boda

Rosa
Kosta/Boda

KOS 2
Kosta/Boda

KOS 3
Kosta/Boda

Mac Guirlang
Kosta/Boda

Prince/Prins
Kosta/Boda

Gustav Adolph
Kosta/Boda

Safir
Kosta/Boda
Fasceted Stem

Princess
Kosta/Boda

Diamond
Kosta/Boda

Lyx
Kosta/Boda

Brilljant
Kosta/Boda

Vincent
Kosta/Boda

Provence
Kosta/Boda

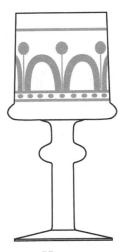

Hussar
Kosta/Boda

Pyramid
Kosta/Boda

Karlberg
Kosta/Boda

Are
Kosta/Boda

Betty
Kosta/Boda

Boden
Kosta/Boda

Doris
Kosta/Boda

Pysen
Kosta/Boda

Mona
Kosta/Boda

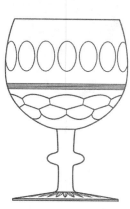

KOS 1
Kosta/Boda

Koskull
Kosta/Boda

Carlton
Kosta/Boda

Suffolk
Kosta/Boda

Kuba
Kosta/Boda

Karen
Kosta/Boda

Solvig
Kosta/Boda

Contessa
Kosta/Boda
Platinum Trim

Spartan
Kosta/Boda

Flora
Kosta/Boda

Grace
Kosta/Boda

Kirsten
Kosta/Boda

Wheat
Kosta/Boda

Bernadotte
Kosta/Boda
Bubble in Stem

171

Isadora
Kosta/Boda
Multicolor Stems

KOS 4
Kosta/Boda

Avon
Kosta/Boda
Bubble Stem

Carole
Kosta/Boda
Ball/Bubble Stem

Reflex
Kosta/Boda

Taylor
Kosta/Boda

Ekeberga
Kosta/Boda

Kronoberg
Kosta/Boda

Cittra
Kosta/Boda

Gina
Kosta/Boda

Martine
Kosta/Boda

Fontain
Kosta/Boda

Romance
Kosta/Boda

Nordic
Kosta/Boda

Rosersberg
Kosta/Boda
Hexagonal Base

Gothenburg
Kosta/Boda

Geraldine
Kosta/Boda

Flach
Kosta/Boda

Florida
Kosta/Boda
Square Base

Solenn II Engraved
Kosta/Boda

Ingrid
Kosta/Boda

Cleopatra
Kosta/Boda

Christmas
Kosta/Boda

Tangent
Kosta/Boda

Viva
Kosta/Boda

Safir
Kosta/Boda
Cut Ball in Stem

Bon Bon
Kosta/Boda
Multicolored

Filippa
Kosta/Boda
Blue

Johansfors
Kosta/Boda
Multicolor Rings

Palm Trees
Kosta/Boda
Multicolor Stem

Gripsholm
Kosta/Boda

Fenix
Kosta/Boda

Epoque
Kosta/Boda
Clear, Colored, or Gold Stem

Amazon
Kosta/Boda
Orange Frosted Stem

Bella Boda
Kosta/Boda
Various Colors

Elvira Madigan
Kosta/Boda

Texas
Kosta/Boda
Blue

Ocean
Kosta/Boda
Turquoise, Blue, or Yellow

Grapes
Kosta/Boda

Mambo
Kosta/Boda
Bubble in Base

Rondo
Kosta/Boda
Bubble in Stem

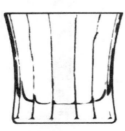

Admiral
Kosta/Boda

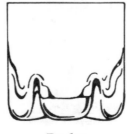

Rocky
Kosta/Boda

Rainbow
Kosta/Boda
Barware

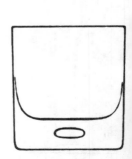

Pippi
Kosta/Boda

Colonade
Kosta/Boda

Samba
Kosta/Boda
Bubble in Base

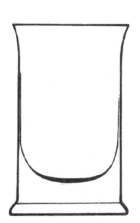

Flagg
Kosta/Boda

KRZ 1
Kristal Zajecar

Belvedere
Kusak
5600

Inspiration
Kusak

Jasmine
Kusak

Leaves
Kusak
5700

Springtime
Kusak
3408

Alger
Lalique

Ange
Lalique

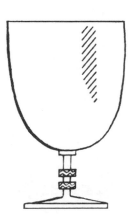

Argos
Lalique

Barsac
Lalique
Frosted Stem

Beaugency
Lalique

Bellini
Lalique

Blois
Lalique
Cut Base

Bourgueil
Lalique

Chéne
Lalique

Chenonceaux
Lalique

Chinon
Lalique

Clos Vougeot
Lalique

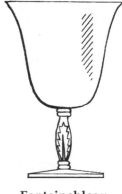

Fontainebleau
Lalique

France
Lalique

Guebwiller
Lalique

Langeais
Lalique

Phalsbourg
Lalique

Rambouillet
Lalique

Roxane
Lalique

Royal
Lalique

Saint Hubert
Lalique

Tosca
Lalique

Treves
Lalique

Tuileries
Lalique

Volnay
Lalique

Flora
Lauffer

Bedford Gold
Ralph Lauren

Edward Gold
Ralph Lauren

Emma
Ralph Lauren

Glen Plaid
Ralph Lauren

Glen Plaid Classic
Ralph Lauren

Herringbone
Ralph Lauren

Herringbone Classic
Ralph Lauren

Landon
Ralph Lauren
Also "Landon Gold"

Lenox Stem Shapes

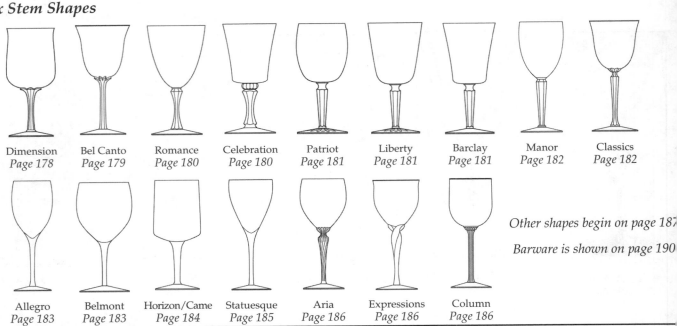

| Dimension
Page 178 | Bel Canto
Page 179 | Romance
Page 180 | Celebration
Page 180 | Patriot
Page 181 | Liberty
Page 181 | Barclay
Page 181 | Manor
Page 182 | Classics
Page 182 |

| Allegro
Page 183 | Belmont
Page 183 | Horizon/Came
Page 184 | Statuesque
Page 185 | Aria
Page 186 | Expressions
Page 186 | Column
Page 186 |

Other shapes begin on page 187

Barware is shown on page 190

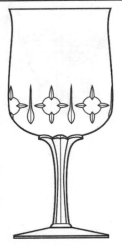

Afterglow
Lenox

Blue Mist
Lenox
Dark Blue

Desire
Lenox
Platinum Trim

Dimension
Lenox

Espresso
Lenox
Brown

Gold Mist
Lenox
Yellow

Green Mist
Lenox
Green

Holiday
Lenox
Older, Gold Trim

Intrigue
Lenox
Gold Trim

Lace Point
Lenox
Platinum Trim

Lilac Mist
Lenox
Purple

Midnight Mood
Lenox
Black

Moonspun
Lenox
Platinum Trim

Pearl Mist
Lenox
Light Smoke

Pendant
Lenox

Plum Blossoms
Lenox
Platinum Trim

Silver Mist
Lenox
Blue/Gray

Wheat
Lenox

White Echo
Lenox
Platinum Trim

Wildflower
Lenox
Platinum Trim

Allure
Lenox

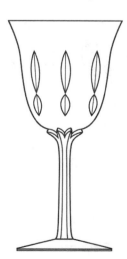

Candlelight
Lenox

Castle Garden
Lenox

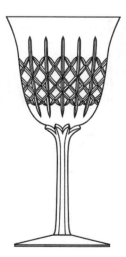

Evening Star
Lenox

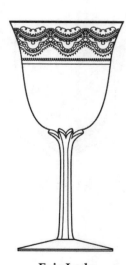

Fair Lady
Lenox
Platinum Trim

Fontaine
Lenox
Gold Trim

Hayworth
Lenox
Gold Trim

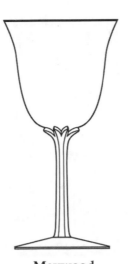

Maywood
Lenox
Platinum Trim

Sky Blossoms
Lenox
Older, Blue Bowl

Sutton Place
Lenox
Black Stem

Temple Blossom
Lenox

Brookdale
Lenox

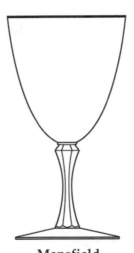

Mansfield
Lenox
Gold Trim

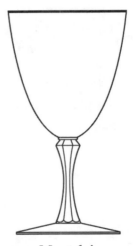

Montclair
Lenox
Platinum Trim

Romance
Lenox

Sapphire
Lenox
Smoke Bowl and Foot

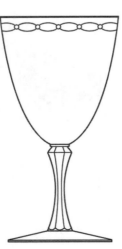

Sentiment
Lenox
Platinum Trim

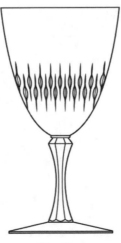

Starfire
Lenox
Older, Romance Shape

Tuxedo
Lenox
Gold Encrusted

Flourish
Lenox

Gala
Lenox

Jubilee
Lenox

Pageant
Lenox

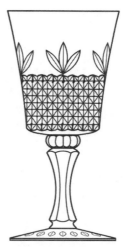

Revelry
Lenox

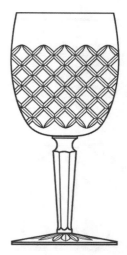

Annapolis
Lenox
Older, Patriot Shape

Monticello
Lenox

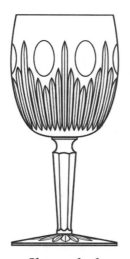

Shenandoah
Lenox

Annapolis
Lenox
Newer, Liberty Shape

Beacon Hill
Lenox

Charleston
Lenox

Charleston Gold
Lenox

Mystic
Lenox

Saratoga
Lenox

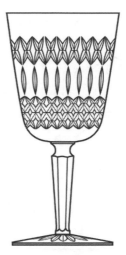

Sequoia
Lenox

Autumn
Lenox
Older, Thin Gold Band

Barclay
Lenox

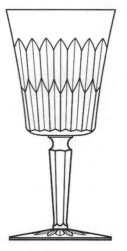

Brilliance
Lenox

Eternal
Lenox
Gold, Barclay Shape

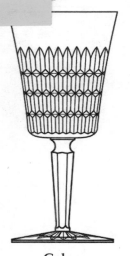

Galaxy
Lenox

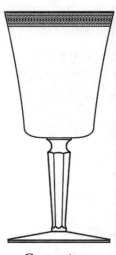

Georgetown
Lenox
Gold Encrusted

Manor
Lenox

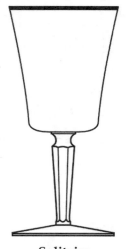

Solitaire
Lenox
Platinum Trim

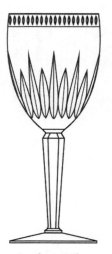

Ambassador
Lenox
Gold Trim

Baltic
Lenox

Centurion
Lenox

Clarity
Lenox

Clarity Gold
Lenox
Gold Trim

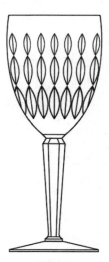

Serene
Lenox

Sterling
Lenox

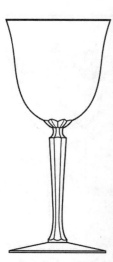

Classic Federal
Lenox
Gold or Platinum Trim

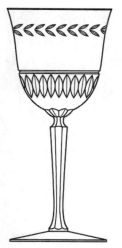

Classic Laurel
Lenox
Gold Trim

Classic Legend
Lenox
Gold Trim

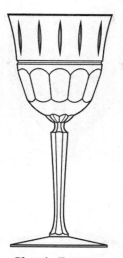

Classic Regency
Lenox
Gold Trim

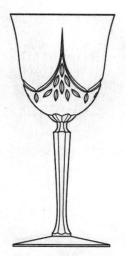

Classic Royalton
Lenox
Gold Trim

Classic Shell
Lenox
Gold or Platinum Trim

Hartwell House
Lenox
Gold Trim

Allegro
Lenox

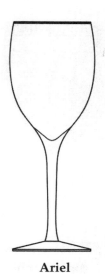

Ariel
Lenox
Platinum Trim

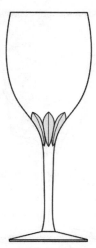

Atrium
Lenox
Frosted Cuts

Crystal Fantasy
Lenox

Eclipse
Lenox
Gold Trim

Starfire
Lenox
Newer, Allegro Shape

Tenderly
Lenox

Tracery
Lenox

Belmont
Lenox

Lenox

Candleglow
Lenox

Blue Rhapsody
Lenox
Blue/Gray

Blue Shadow
Lenox
Blue, Platinum Trim

Dusk Shadow
Lenox
Brown, Gold Trim

Evening Shadow
Lenox
Black, Platinum Trim

Green Shadow
Lenox
Green, Platinum Trim

Laurent
Lenox
Gold Trim

Plum Shadow
Lenox
Purple, Platinum Trim

Radiance
Lenox

Royale
Lenox
Gold Encrusted

Silver Shadow
Lenox
Blue/Gray, Platinum Trim

Springdale
Lenox
Platinum Trim

Twilight Shadow
Lenox
Smoke, Platinum Trim

Weatherly
Lenox
Platinum Trim

Blue Smoke
Lenox
Blue Bowl and Foot

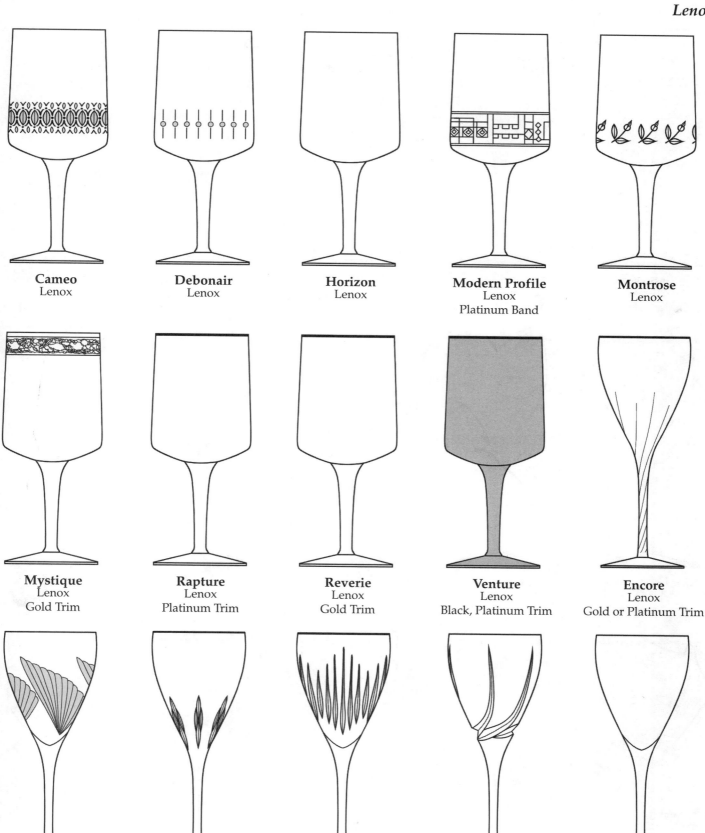

Cameo
Lenox

Debonair
Lenox

Horizon
Lenox

Modern Profile
Lenox
Platinum Band

Montrose
Lenox

Mystique
Lenox
Gold Trim

Rapture
Lenox
Platinum Trim

Reverie
Lenox
Gold Trim

Venture
Lenox
Black, Platinum Trim

Encore
Lenox
Gold or Platinum Trim

Fanlight
Lenox
Frosted Cutting

Firelight
Lenox
Plain or with Gold or Plat. Trim

Grandeur
Lenox
Gold Trim

Sea Swirl
Lenox

Statuesque
Lenox

Lenox

Statuesque
Lenox
Optic, Gold Trim

Twilight
Lenox
Plain or with Gold Trim

Windswept
Lenox

Aria
Lenox

Citation Gold
Lenox

Domaine
Lenox
Cut, Gold Trim

Holiday
Lenox
Newer, Gold Encrusted

Madison
Lenox
PlatinumTrim

Monroe
Lenox
Gold Trim

Elegance
Lenox
Platinum Trim

Embrace
Lenox
Frosted Stem

Rhythm
Lenox
Gold or Platinum Trim

Unity
Lenox
Gold Trim

Autumn
Lenox
Newer, Wide Gold Band

Fillmore
Lenox
Platinum Trim

Kingston
Lenox
Platinum Trim

Liberty
Lenox
Gold Trim

McKinley
Lenox
Gold Trim

Charlotte
Lenox

Hanover
Lenox

Amelia
Lenox

Lenox Charter
Lenox

Lenox Masterpiece
Lenox

Decor Cut
Lenox
Hotelware

Decor Optic
Lenox
Hotelware

Decor Plain
Lenox
Hotelware

Debut
Lenox

Debut Gold
Lenox
Gold Trim

Erica
Lenox
Gold Trim

Erin
Lenox
Platinum Trim

Lenox

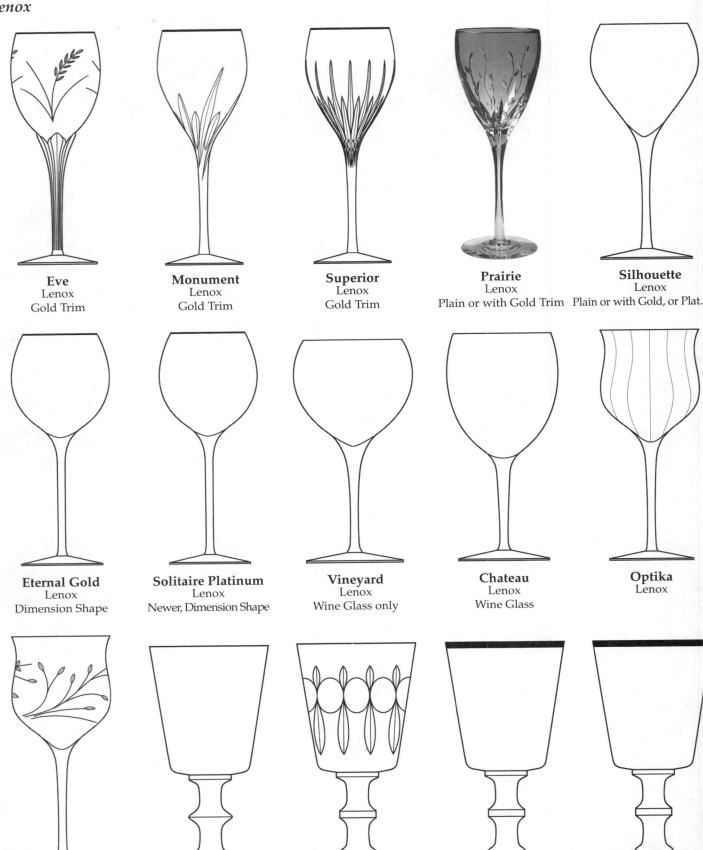

Eve
Lenox
Gold Trim

Monument
Lenox
Gold Trim

Superior
Lenox
Gold Trim

Prairie
Lenox
Plain or with Gold Trim

Silhouette
Lenox
Plain or with Gold, or Plat.

Eternal Gold
Lenox
Dimension Shape

Solitaire Platinum
Lenox
Newer, Dimension Shape

Vineyard
Lenox
Wine Glass only

Chateau
Lenox
Wine Glass

Optika
Lenox

Somerset
Lenox

Embassy House
Lenox

Aristocrat
Lenox

Diplomat
Lenox
Platinum Trim

Viceroy
Lenox
Gold Trim

Ensemble
Lenox
Blush (pink) or Cobalt

Bluebell
Lenox
Blue, Tempo Line

Buttercup
Lenox
Yellow, Tempo Line

Emerald
Lenox
Green, Tempo Line

Icicle
Lenox
Clear, Tempo Line

Nutmeg
Lenox
Brown, Tempo Line

Dawn Blossoms
Lenox
Pink

Day Blossoms
Lenox
Clear

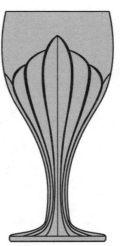

Sky Blossoms
Lenox
Newer, Dark Blue

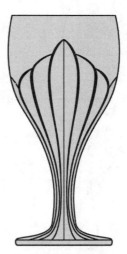

Twilight Blossoms
Lenox
Medium Blue

Impromptu
Lenox
Various Colors

Navarre
Lenox
Clear, Blue, or Pink

Alexandra
Lenox
Frosted Fern

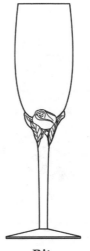

Ritz
Lenox
Fluted Champagne Only

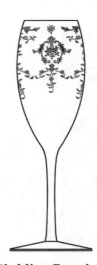

Wedding Promises
Lenox
Fluted Champagne Only

Antique
Lenox
Various Colors

Casual
Lenox
Various Colors

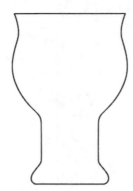

Clarion
Lenox
Various Colors

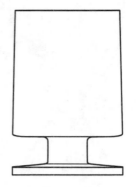

Summit
Lenox

Olympic
Lenox
Imperial Barware

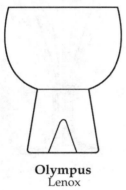

Olympus
Lenox

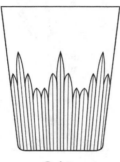

Orion
Lenox
Galaxy Barware

Pegasus
Lenox
Galaxy Barware

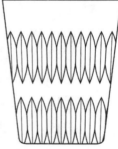

Polaris
Lenox
Galaxy Barware

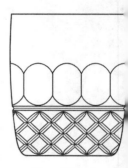

Providence
Lenox
Concord Barware

Tartan
Lenox
Barware

Turkey Eagle
Lenox
Barware

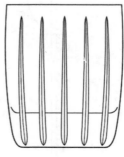

Starfire
Lenox
Concord Barware

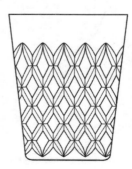

Starfire
Lenox
Galaxy Barware

Capella
Lenox
Galaxy Barware

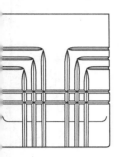

Deco
Lenox
Barware

1001-3
Libbey/Rock Sharpe

1004-3
Libbey/Rock Sharpe

1004-4
Libbey/Rock Sharpe

1007-5
Libbey/Rock Sharpe

1013-4
Libbey/Rock Sharpe

1023-2
Libbey/Rock Sharpe

1023-3
Libbey/Rock Sharpe

2003-2
Libbey/Rock Sharpe

2006-4
Libbey/Rock Sharpe

2008-4
Libbey/Rock Sharpe

2008-5
Libbey/Rock Sharpe

2009-10
Libbey/Rock Sharpe

2010-8
Libbey/Rock Sharpe

2010-9
Libbey/Rock Sharpe

Libbey/Rock Sharpe

2011-16
Libbey/Rock Sharpe

2011-17
Libbey/Rock Sharpe

2011-18
Libbey/Rock Sharpe

2011-19
Libbey/Rock Sharpe

2014-3
Libbey/Rock Sharp

3001-4
Libbey/Rock Sharpe

3003-6
Libbey/Rock Sharpe

3003-7
Libbey/Rock Sharpe

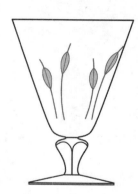

3004-1
Libbey/Rock Sharpe

3004-2
Libbey/Rock Sharp

3005-18
Libbey/Rock Sharpe

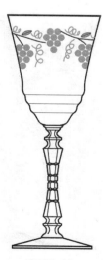

3005-19
Libbey/Rock Sharpe

3006-12
Libbey/Rock Sharpe

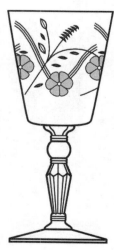

3006-13
Libbey/Rock Sharpe

3006-14
Libbey/Rock Sharp

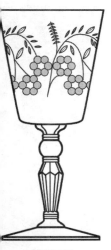

3006-15
Libbey/Rock Sharpe

3007-7
Libbey/Rock Sharpe

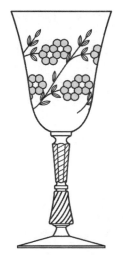

3007-8
Libbey/Rock Sharpe

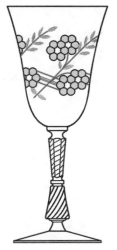

3007-9
Libbey/Rock Sharpe

3010-1
Libbey/Rock Sharpe

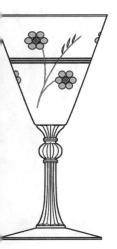

3010-2
Libbey/Rock Sharpe

Milam
Libbey/Rock Sharpe
1001

Westminster
Libbey/Rock Sharpe
1002

Patrician
Lobmeyer
Gold Lustre

Pavie
Lorraine

Poitiers
Lorraine

Valmy
Lorraine

MCB 1
McBride

MCB 2
McBride
Blue Base

Antique Lace
Mikasa
T2715, Gold Trim

193

Belle Terre
Mikasa
T2718

Jamestown
Mikasa
T2700

Jamestown
Mikasa
Gold or Platinum Trim

Jamestown
Mikasa
Ruby

Merrick
Mikasa (Iced Tea)
Etched Flowers, Gold

Monticello
Mikasa
Gold Trim

Ribbon Holly
Mikasa
T2722, Gold Trim, Decal

Royal Jamestown
Mikasa
T2723, Gold Accent

Silk Flowers
Mikasa
T2720, Decal

Sorrento
Mikasa
T2717

Tea Rose
Mikasa

Antique Lace
Mikasa
91246, Cut

Lyric
Mikasa
91247, Older

Melody
Mikasa
91249, Older

Queen Anne
Mikasa
91245

Rhapsody
Mikasa
91242

Sonata
Mikasa
91253

Sonnet
Mikasa
91241, Older

Summer Song
Mikasa
91244

Symphony
Mikasa
91243

Old Dublin
Mikasa
SN110

Autumn Vale
Mikasa
91352

Caress
Mikasa
91344

Crescendo
Mikasa
91349

Embrace
Mikasa
91350

Eternal
Mikasa
91355

Heritage
Mikasa
91301

Shadow
Mikasa
91351

Tenderly
Mikasa
91345

Wind Swept
Mikasa
91353

Mikasa

Belvedere
Mikasa
91146

Cambridge
Mikasa
91143

Candlelight
Mikasa
91150

Coronation
Mikasa
91140, Older

Lafayette
Mikasa
91144, Older

Savoy
Mikasa
91100

Stratford
Mikasa
91147

Twin Oaks
Mikasa

Wimbledon
Mikasa
91142

Paris
Mikasa
Various Colors

Ashley
Mikasa
TS107

Briarcliffe
Mikasa
TS102, Platinum

Bryn Mawr
Mikasa
TS105

Chatsworth
Mikasa
TS112

Claridge
Mikasa
TS111

196

Coventry
Mikasa
TS104

Inspiration
Mikasa
TS113

Interlude
Mikasa
TS110

Kingsley
Mikasa
TS103

Larchmont
Mikasa
TS108

Park Avenue
Mikasa
TS115

Vanderbilt
Mikasa
TS114

Wheaton
Mikasa
TS101, Gold Trim

Icicles
Mikasa
SN130

Cathay
Mikasa
40124, Gold Trim

Dune Grass
Mikasa
40128, Older

Illusion
Mikasa
40100

Innovation
Mikasa
40126

Meadow Song
Mikasa
40130

Moonglow
Mikasa
40107, Platinum Trim

Spun Gold
Mikasa
40105, Gold Trim

Sutton Point
Mikasa
40132

Arabesque
Mikasa
40225

Ballet
Mikasa
40205

Plie
Mikasa
40226

Ardmore
Mikasa
40001

Brocade
Mikasa
40017, Gold Trim

Canterbury
Mikasa
40065

Cathedral
Mikasa
40060

Chambray
Mikasa
40069

Chateau
Mikasa
40063

Gold Crown
Mikasa
40061, Gold Trim

Laura
Mikasa
40007, Frosted Stem

Montclair
Mikasa
40066

Normandy
Mikasa
40068

Nymphenburg
Mikasa

Versailles
Mikasa
40062

Classic Flair
Mikasa
T7312, Decal

Napoli
Mikasa
Gold or Platinum Trim

Trousseau
Mikasa
T7317, Newer, Gold

Cameo
Mikasa
57640

Crown Jewels
Mikasa
57625

Empire
Mikasa
57621, Gold Trim

Just Flowers
Mikasa
57626

Regency
Mikasa
57620, Platinum Bands

Silver Mist
Mikasa
57618, Platinum Trim

Interlude
Mikasa
57940

September Song
Mikasa
57926

Seville
Mikasa
59000, Optic

Marquis
Mikasa
SN1057840

Medici
Mikasa
23141

Spectrum
Mikasa
T2102, aka "Everest"

Sonata
Mikasa
T7102, Gold Trim

Sonnet
Mikasa
Various Colors

Sonnet Platinum
Mikasa
Platinum Trim

Flair
Mikasa
T2202, Clear

Gramercy
Mikasa
Various Colors

Kensington
Mikasa
T1000

Dorset
Mikasa
T1102

Westminster
Mikasa
T1101

Windsor
Mikasa
T1100

Ascot
Mikasa
T1200

Berkshire
Mikasa
T1202

MIC3
Mikasa

Buckingham
Mikasa
XY816

Castille Gold
Mikasa
XY818

Golden Palace
Mikasa
XY815, Gold Trim

Imperial Gold
Mikasa
XY814, Gold Trim

Mystic Meadow
Mikasa
XY819

Resplenda
Mikasa
XY813

Resplenda Gold
Mikasa
XY812, Gold Trim

Splendor
Mikasa
XY811

Touch of Spring
Mikasa
XY810

Crescendo
Mikasa
Gold Trim

Paramount
Mikasa

Regency
Mikasa
Gold Trim

Wisteria
Mikasa
XYM01

Uptown
Mikasa
SN104

Apollo
Mikasa
SN113

Covent Garden
Mikasa
SN116

Mikasa

Golden Tiara
Mikasa
SN121, Gold Trim

Tiara
Mikasa
SN120

Borealis
Mikasa
XYJ10

Diamonds
Mikasa
XYJ66

Dubarry
Mikasa
XYJ11

Dynasty
Mikasa
XYJ12

Rendezvous Gold
Mikasa
Cut, also without Gold

Sauvignon
Mikasa
XYJ17

Sonora
Mikasa
XYJ16

Arctic Lights
Mikasa
XY701

Provincial Gold
Mikasa
XYJ13

Bacchus
Mikasa
XY720

Barcelona
Mikasa
XY713

Calla Lily
Mikasa
XY711

English Garden
Mikasa
XY708

Firelight
Mikasa
XY705

Flame D' Amore
Mikasa
XY714

Glade
Mikasa
XY709

Golden Lights
Mikasa
XY746, Gold Trim

Moonbeams
Mikasa
XY702

Northern Lights
Mikasa
XY710

Noveau
Mikasa
XY706

Olympus
Mikasa
XY703

Petite Points
Mikasa
XY718

Preview Gold
Mikasa
XY733, Gold Trim

Rambling Rose
Mikasa
XY726

Symmetry
Mikasa
XY704

Tiger Lily
Mikasa
XY707

Mardi Gras
Mikasa
XY730

Phoenix
Mikasa
XY725

Mikasa

Baronet
Mikasa
XYJ68, also with Gold Trim

Chantilly
Mikasa
XYJ73

Corinthian
Mikasa
XYJ72

Coronation
Mikasa
XYJ51, Newer

Corsica
Mikasa
XYJ58

Duchessa
Mikasa
XYJ54

Fiero
Mikasa
XYJ60

Karma
Mikasa
XYJ74

Kismet
Mikasa
XYJ69

Manor House
Mikasa
XYJ65, Gold Trim

Palomino
Mikasa
XYJ64

Amherst
Mikasa
60940, Champagne Flute

Infinity
Mikasa
61036

Toselli
Mikasa
61053

Lyric
Mikasa
T7002, Gold Trim

Melody
Mikasa
T7001, Newer, Optic

Stephanie
Mikasa
T7201, also with Gold Trim

Nicole
Mikasa
T7200

Midas Gold
Mikasa
TZ003, Gold Trim

Venice
Mikasa
T1300-001, Studio Nova

Murano
Mikasa
T7560

Elegant/Elegance
Mikasa
Various Colors

Elite
Mikasa
Various Colors

Sweet Melody
Mikasa
XYD11

Venetian
Mikasa
XYD10

Venetian Gold
Mikasa
XYD12, Gold Trim

Radiance
Mikasa

Rivoli
Mikasa
Various Colors

Clarion
Mikasa
40501

Clarion
Mikasa
40532, Gold Trim

Simplicity
Mikasa
55001

September Song
Mikasa
55041

Chelsea
Mikasa
20341

Aegean Mist
Mikasa
XYS03

Brittany
Mikasa
XYS04

Dune Grass
Mikasa
Newer, XYS02

Lido
Mikasa
Various Colors

Noir
Mikasa
SX775, Black

Calla Lilies
Mikasa
SX110, Frosted Decals

Charisma
Mikasa
SX111

Classique
Mikasa
SX100

Starburst
Mikasa
SX105

Silver Surf
Mikasa
SX103

Venetian Opal
Mikasa
25588

Laguna
Mikasa
23231, Frosted Stem

Gloria
Mikasa
SX502

Saturn
Mikasa
SX500, Frosted Stem

Sophisticate
Mikasa
SX701, Gold Trim

Grand Prix
Mikasa
11741

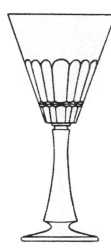

Sutton Place
Mikasa
11740

Wind Drift
Mikasa
11726

Bon Vivant
Mikasa
58717, Frosted Stem

Crystal Waves
Mikasa
XYC60

Dew Drop
Mikasa
XYC61

Embassy Hall
Mikasa
XYC52

Imperial Palace
Mikasa
XYC05

Medley
Mikasa
XYC04

Mystique
Mikasa
XYC06, Frosted Stem

New Horizon
Mikasa
XYC01

Palace Ring
Mikasa
XYC53

Papyrus
Mikasa
XYC08

Symphony
Mikasa
XYC02

Tuxedo
Mikasa
XYC07

Windsor Park
Mikasa
XYC03

Braid
Mikasa
SX725

Criss Cross
Mikasa
SXM03

Moonspun
Mikasa
59921, Platinum Trim

Solitaire
Mikasa
59900/SXM00

Vista
Mikasa
59930/SXM01

Academy
Mikasa
RKA02, Black & Gold Acc

Hyde Park
Mikasa
29100

Just Love
Mikasa
RKA07

South Hampton
Mikasa
RKA01, Gold Trim

Grimaldi
Mikasa
12741

Trianon
Mikasa
12640, Older

Excelsior
Mikasa
XZ001

Aida
Mikasa
60124

Helena
Mikasa
60129

Luna
Mikasa
Gold or Platinum Trim

Belaire
Mikasa
91001

Crown Princess
Mikasa
91043

Fair Lady
Mikasa
91041

Sovereign
Mikasa
91042

Viscount
Mikasa
91040

Buckingham
Mikasa
11046

Edinburgh
Mikasa
11045

Manor House
Mikasa
10447, Older

Foliage
Mikasa
91431

Heirloom
Mikasa
91401

Lacy Fern
Mikasa
91426

Spring Petals
Mikasa
T7410

Romanaire
Mikasa
T7412

Firenze
Mikasa
Frosted Stem

Deco
Mikasa
26310, Various Colors

Ambiance
Mikasa
Various Colors

Monte Carlo
Mikasa
T2000/403, Studio Nova

Monaco
Mikasa
T2001, Studio Nova

Enchantress
Mikasa
RRB00

Promises
Mikasa
RR001

MIC4
Mikasa

Galleria
Mikasa
Various Colors

Monarch
Mikasa
Frosted Butterfly

Mariposa
Mikasa
Various Colors

Bridal Veil
Mikasa
RKB00, Frosted Stem

Primavera
Mikasa
XYR00

Pirouette
Mikasa
26210

Palladium
Mikasa
Various Colors

Fleurisse
Mikasa
Various Colors

Classic Flair
Mikasa
Various Colors

Rapture
Mikasa
32521, Gold Filled

Sea Mist
Mikasa
Various Colors

Fiore
Mikasa
23417, Frosted Petals

Prisma
Mikasa

Blossom
Mikasa
Various Colors

Vogue
Mikasa
Black or Frosted Stem

Skyline
Mikasa
Various Colors, Optic

Pyramid
Mikasa
SXE07, Black Stem

First Love
Mikasa
SX302

Latitude
Mikasa

Belladonna
Mikasa
292, Various Colors

Mikasa

Tulip
Mikasa
Various Colors

Fleurette
Mikasa
Various Colors

Flower Song
Mikasa
58300

La Belle
Mikasa
TS502

La Dame
Mikasa
TS503, Frosted Stem

L'Amour
Mikasa
T7500

Horizon
Mikasa
40922, Frosted Stem

Perspective
Mikasa
40903

Vision
Mikasa
40932, Gold Trim

MIC1
Mikasa

Talia
Mikasa/Christopher Stuart
Plain or with Gold Trim

Berkeley
Mikasa
SN108

Malibu
Mikasa
SN115

Park Lane
Mikasa
SN101

The Ritz
Mikasa
TS400

Stratton
Mikasa
TS450

Regal Hall
Mikasa
TS609, Frosted Stem

Royal Manor
Mikasa
TS600

Richelieu
Mikasa
SN112

Parthenon
Mikasa
T7550

Cameo
Mikasa
Christopher Stuart

Christmas Tree
Mikasa
SN106

Contempo
Mikasa
T2900

Finesse
Mikasa
T3500

Domino
Mikasa
SXG01

Geometry
Mikasa
SXH01

Ashford
Mikasa
26841, Gold Trim

Eclipse
Mikasa

Reflections
Mikasa

Elysee
Mikasa
SXF07, Black Stem

Ciara
Mikasa
Various Colors

Charleston
Mikasa
SXT01

French Countryside
Mikasa
TYC01

Country French
Mikasa
Various Colors

Triomphe
Mikasa
Various Colored Stems

English Countryside
Mikasa
Various Colors

Estate
Mikasa
Various Colors

French Twist
Mikasa
Various Colors

Terrace
Mikasa
Various Colors

Summit
Mikasa

Intermezzo
Mikasa
23500

Fontaine
Mikasa
SN109

Promenade
Mikasa
X1211, Various Colors

Memory
Mikasa

Prism
Mikasa
91502

Pearls
Mikasa
T4050

Pearls Gold
Mikasa
Gold Ball, also Pearls Ebony

Penthouse
Mikasa
58200

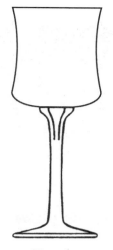

Tuxedo
Mikasa

Frost Fire
Mikasa
58417

Royal Crown
Mikasa
Various Colors

Grand Table
Mikasa
Black Stem, Burgundy

Continental
Mikasa
T2800

Ambassador
Mikasa
RT103, Barware

Ascot Park
Mikasa
40907, Barware

Currents
Mikasa
XY742, Highball

Executive Suite
Mikasa
TO100, Barware

Fairhaven
Mikasa
SN103

Le Grand Fleur
Mikasa
T4101, Highball

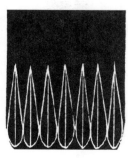

Marquette
Mikasa
RT108, Barware

Pageant
Mikasa
XY743, Barware

Plaza Suite
Mikasa
40906, Barware

Polygon
Mikasa
RT115, Barware

Reflections
Mikasa
XYW03, Barware

Trianon
Mikasa
XYW04, Frosted Cut

Triumph
Mikasa
RT116, Barware

Wilshire
Mikasa
SN102, Barware

Rainbow
Mila International
Various Colors

Brocade
Mirabell

Charm
Mirabell
Also with Gold or Platinum

Simone
Moncrief
Platinum

Arlene
Monongah
6102, Cut 655

Bo Peep
Monongah
6102, Etch 854

Maxwell
Monongah
6120, Cut 660

Roseland
Monongah
7814, Etch 900

Springtime
Monongah
845, Plain or with Gold

MNN 1
Monongahela

MNN 2
Monongahela

Golf Ball
Morgantown
7643, Various Colors

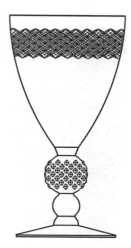

Avon
Morgantown
7643

Eton
Morgantown
7643

7643-1
Morgantown
7643

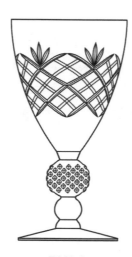

7643-2
Morgantown
7643

7643-3
Morgantown
7643

7643-4
Morgantown
7643

Old English
Morgantown
7678, Colored Bowl

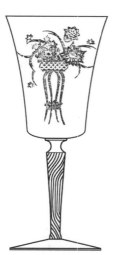

Nantucket
Morgantown
7654, Etch 766

Sunrise Medallion
Morgantown
7654 ½, Etch 758

Empress
Morgantown
7660 ½

Majesty
Morgantown
7662, Ruby Bowl

217

Georgian
Morgantown
7667

Elizabeth
Morgantown
7664, Etch 757

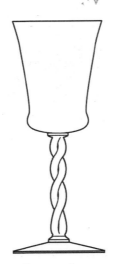

Queen Ann
Morgantown
7664

Sunrise Medallion
Morgantown
7664, Etch 758

Faun
Morgantown
7642, Gold Encrusted

Carlton Marco
Morgantown
7653, Plat. Dec. 31

Monroe
Morgantown
7690, Colored Bowl

Saranac
Morgantown
7690

Stem 7691
Morgantown

Monica
Morgantown
7691

7691-1
Morgantown
7691

7691-2
Morgantown
7691

7630-1
Morgantown
7630

Sunrise Medallion
Morgantown
7630, Etch 758

Cathay
Morgantown
7668, Etch 811

Lace Bouquet
Morgantown
7668, Etch 810

Mayfair
Morgantown
7668, Etch 787 ½

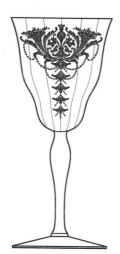

Milan
Morgantown
7668, Etch 778

Mayfair
Morgantown
7711, Etch 787 ½

Mikado
Morgantown
7711, Etch 808

Versailles
Morgantown
7711, Etch 795

Virginia
Morgantown
7711, Etch 733

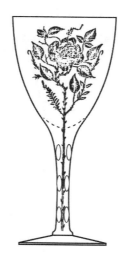

American Beauty
Morgantown
7565, Etch 734

Morgana
Morgantown
7577, Gold Dec. 329

Primrose Lane
Morgantown
7577, Etch 329

Biscayne
Morgantown
7586, Gold Encrusted

7586-1
Morgantown
7586, Gold Encrusted

Carlton Marco
Morgantown
7604 ½, Gold Encrusted

Queen Louise
Morgantown
7614

Radiant
Morgantown
7685, Blue or Ruby

219

7685-1
Morgantown
7685

Starlight
Morgantown

Sextette
Morgantown
7703

Carlton
Morgantown
7606 ½, Black

Brilliant
Morgantown
7617

Kyoto
Morgantown
21493AN, Etch 760

Plantation
Morgantown
8445, Colored Bowl

Art Moderne
Morgantown
7640, Black Stem

Victoria Regina
Morgantown
7640

Fernlee
Morgantown
7695, Etch 785

Fire & Ice
Morgantown
6060, Red Foot

President's House
Morgantown
7780

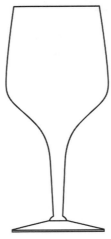

Vision
Morgantown
3008, Various Colors

Regina
Morgantown
Pink

Patriot
Morgantown
3014, Various Colors

Swirl
Morgantown
9844, Square Base

Thumbprint
Morgantown
9872, Various Colors

Crinkle
Morgantown
1962, Various Colors

American Modern
Morgantown
Various Colors

Montego
Morgantown
3011

Jockey
Morgantown
Amber Bowl

Copenhagen
Moser
9900, Gold Encrusted

Lady Hamilton
Moser
15000, Gold Trim

Maharani
Moser
4400, Gold Trim

Mozart
Moser
18280

Pope
Moser
11520

Rose
Moser, 7000
Engraved, Gold Inlay and Trim

Royal
Moser
9000, Gold Trim

Splendid
Moser
10160, Gold Encrusted

Alexandra
Nachtmann

Andernach
Nachtmann

Angelique
Nachtmann

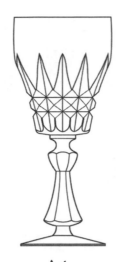

Astra
Nachtmann

Bamburg
Nachtmann

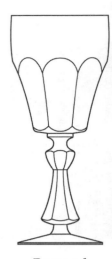

Burgund
Nachtmann

Contessa
Nachtmann

Diabolo
Nachtmann

Dora
Nachtmann
Cordial

Fleurie
Nachtmann

Lady
Nachtmann

Libelle
Nachtmann

Nierstein
Nachtmann

Opal
Nachtmann

Patrizia
Nachtmann

Sonja
Nachtmann

Stefanie
Nachtmann

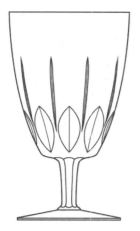

Sylvia
Nachtmann

Tiffany
Nachtmann

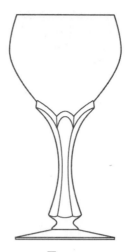

Topas
Nachtmann

Traube
Nachtmann
Various Colors

Adagio
Noritake

Blue Hill
Noritake

Carolyn
Noritake

Heritage
Noritake
Gold Trim

Ranier
Noritake

Spectrum
Noritake
Platinum Trim

Tahoe
Noritake

Anticipation
Noritake

Gallery
Noritake

Gold & Platinum
Noritake

Morning Jewel
Noritake
Gold Trim

Paris
Noritake
Platinum Trim

Patience
Noritake

Remembrance
Noritake
Various Colors

Troy
Noritake
Gold Trim

Virtue
Noritake

Salutation
Noritake
Gold Trim

Golden Tribute
Noritake
Gold Trim

Royal Orchid
Noritake
Clear or Pink

Royal Pierpont
Noritake
Clear, Blue, Pink, or Gra

Sterling Tribute
Noritake
Platinum Trim

Admiration
Noritake
Gold Trim

Buckingham
Noritake
Platinum Trim

Aquarius
Noritake
Blue Bowl

Cut 818
Noritake
Platinum Trim

Harriet
Noritake

Nocturne
Noritake

Rainbow
Noritake
Various Colors

Rainbow
Noritake
Colored, Plat. Trim

Rhythm
Noritake
Platinum Trim

Rondo
Noritake

Windswept
Noritake

Bouquet
Noritake

Cascade
Noritake

Celestial
Noritake
Gold Trim

Contemporary
Noritake

Cut 814
Noritake

Duet
Noritake

Hope
Noritake

Primrose
Noritake

Promenade
Noritake

Reginald
Noritake

Simplicity
Noritake
Platinum Trim

Sweet Home
Noritake

D'Orsay
Noritake

Dartmoor
Noritake

Fascination
Noritake
Gold Trim

Imagination
Noritake
Platinum Trim

Focus
Noritake
Various Colors

Courtly
Noritake

Esteem
Noritake

Heritage
Noritake

Kenley
Noritake

Hampton Hall
Noritake

Lasalle
Noritake

Memoir
Noritake

Westerleigh
Noritake

Vendome
Noritake
Also with Gold Trim

Aston
Noritake

Benevolence
Noritake

Illumination
Noritake

Madison Ave.
Noritake

Moondust
Noritake

Turning Point
Noritake

Vista
Noritake
Various Colors

Aquitaine
Noritake
Gold and Platinum Trim

Monde D'Or
Noritake
Gold Encrusted

Juliet
Noritake
Platinum Trim

Lorelei
Noritake
Platinum Trim

Pasadena
Noritake
Platinum Trim

Noritake

Romeo
Noritake
Gold Trim

Crystal Cove
Noritake

Masters
Noritake

Rothschild
Noritake

Fiori
Noritake

Persona
Noritake

Positano
Noritake

Resplendent
Noritake
Clear or Pink

Bamboo
Noritake

Viewpoint
Noritake
Various Colors

Novus
Noritake
Various Colors

Perspective
Noritake
Various Colors

Provincial
Noritake
Various Colors

Spotlight
Noritake
Various Colors

Entree
Noritake
Various Colors

Strawberry Delight
Noritake
Light Blue

Sweet Swirl
Noritake
Various Colors

Arbor
Noritake
Various Colors

Britta
Notsjoe

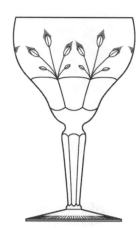

Martha
Oertel Glass
2316/226

Sunburst
Oerthe

Fedora
Oneida
Optic

Fire Dance Gold
Oneida

Mignon
Oneida
Frosted Cut

Tosca
Oneida
Gold or Platinum Trim

Bancroft
Oneida

Julliard
Oneida

Chandelier
Oneida

Minx
Oneida
Various Colors

Minx
Oneida
Colors with Gold or Plat.

Oneida

Santa Mesa
Oneida

Chateau Gold
Oneida

Toujours
Oneida

Countess
Oneida

Kenwood
Oneida

Mirage
Oneida

Omni
Oneida

Wintersong Gold
Oneida

Ashley
Oneida

Madelon
Oneida

Donizetti
Oneida

Modern Art
Oneida
Champagne Flute

Pretiosa
Oneida
Champagne Flute

Awakening Gold
Oneida

Fontaine
Oneida

Saturn
Oneida

Alouette
Oneida

Downing Street
Oneida

Begonia
Oneida

Belcourt Gold
Oneida

Heiress Gold
Oneida

Solar
Oneida
Frosted Stem

Southern Garden
Oneida

Cascade
Orrefors
Cut Bowl

Esprit
Orrefors
5850, Platinum Trim

Ethereal
Orrefors
5850, Gray, Platinum

Rhapsody
Orrefors
Clear or Smoke

Sea Mist
Orrefors
Gray, Cut Bowl

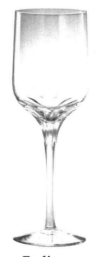

Radiance
Orrefors

Solitude
Orrefors

Claire
Orrefors

Harmony
Orrefors
aka "Blanche"

Lisa
Orrefors

Grace
Orrefors
Faceted Stem

Grace
Orrefors
1652, Smooth Stem

Elisabeth
Orrefors

Antiqua
Orrefors

Susan
Orrefors

Julia
Orrefors
Clear or Smoke

Lisbet
Orrefors

Fantasy
Orrefors
Gray

Illusion
Orrefors

Prelude
Orrefors
Clear

Prelude
Orrefors
Smoke, aka "Adagio"

Starfire
Orrefors
Blue, Platinum Trim

Laura
Orrefors
aka "Play of Lines"

Optica
Orrefors

Crescendo
Orrefors

Diva/Anna
Orrefors

Vintage
Orrefors

Intermezzo
Orrefors
Blue, Black, or Green

Chianti
Orrefors

Caprice
Orrefors
Clear

Mirabel
Orrefors
Smoke

Carina
Orrefors

Maria
Orrefors

Victoria
Orrefors

Helena
Orrefors

Vision
Orrefors
Frosted

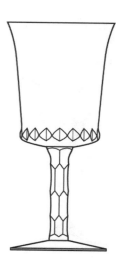

ORR 3
Orrefors

ORR 1
Orrefors

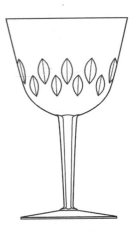

Imperial
Orrefors
HA 2015

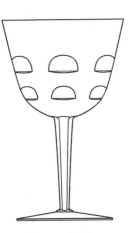

Bernadotte
Orrefors

Karolina
Orrefors

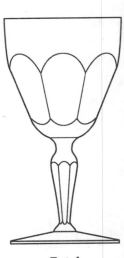

Petal
Orrefors

Annika
Orrefors

Charlotte
Orrefors

Silvia
Orrefors
aka "Mona"

ORR 4
Orrefors

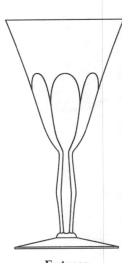

Entress
Orrefors

Gate
Orrefors

Carillon
Orrefors

Symphony
Orrefors

Sven
Orrefors
NC 1688

Drop
Orrefors

Coronation
Orrefors

Sahara
Orrefors

Queen
Orrefors
Blue or Gold

Erika
Orrefors
Clear

Pepperoni
Orrefors
Various Colors

Imperial
Orrefors
Blue, Gold Stars

Eva
Orrefors
Clear or Brown

Anne
Orrefors
Twisted Stem

Berit
Orrefors

Ballet
Orrefors

Contour
Orrefors
Gray

Alice
Orrefors
Clear with Blue Base

Erika
Orrefors
2420, Amber

Ingrid
Orrefors
5420, Platinum Trim

Linnea
Orrefors
Pink Flowers

Orrefors

Maja
Orrefors
Blue Bands, Pink Flo.

Column
Orrefors

ORR 2
Orrefors

Picnic
Orrefors, Colored
2339, aka "Student"

Festival
Orrefors
2338, 4 Colors

London
Orrefors

Karin
Orrefors

Matta
Orrefors
aka "Margit"

Boheme
Orrefors
Clear

Gourmet
Orrefors
Gray

Baltic
Orrefors

Eric
Orrefors

Gustav Adolf
Orrefors

Melody
Orrefors

Eden
Orrefors

Vasa
Orrefors

3101
Orrefors

Spiral
Orrefors

Karl
Orrefors
1545, Barware

Odyssey
Orrefors
Iced Tea

Erik
Orrefors
Barware

Sven
Orrefors
2413, Barware

Calais
Oscar de la Renta
T7360

Cathedral
Oscar de la Renta
Champagne Flute

Chardonnay
Oscar de la Renta
Plain or with Gold Trim

Dresden
Oscar de la Renta
Gold Trim

Lafayette
Oscar de la Renta
T7350

Lafayette
Oscar de la Renta
Gold or Platinum Trim

Le Christophe
Oscar de la Renta

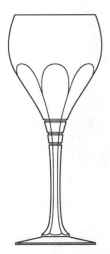

Le Grand Fleur
Oscar de la Renta

Tulipe D'Or
Oscar de la Renta
Gold Band

Tuxedo Gold
Oscar de la Renta
RKC01

Waldorf
Oscar de la Renta
T5004

Wedding Band
Oscar de la Renta
Gold Trim, Frosted

Penny
Paden City Glass
Various Colors

Carol
Pairpoint
185

Coburn
Pairpoint
189

Aurelia
Pasco
Gold Trim

Elmwood
Pasco

Goldenwood
Pasco
Gold Trim

Marvel
Pasco

Rockwood
Pasco

Sterling
Pasco
Platinum Trim

Sunburst
Pasco

Surprise
Pasco

Westwood
Pasco
Platinum Trim

Winthrop
Pasco
Platinum Trim

Wonderful
Pasco

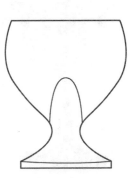

021
Peill

Alexa
Peill
079

Atlantis
Peill

Cora
Peill
Clear or Smoke Bowl

Diana
Peill
124

Domino
Peill

Granada
Peill
195

Iris
Peill

Julia
Peill

Lenore
Peill

Marion
Peill

Malta
Peill
181

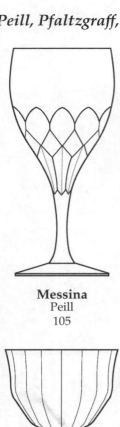

Messina
Peill
105

Pfalzgraf
Peill

Rheinland
Peill
017

Theresa
Peill

Toccata
Peill
063

Vienna
Peill

American Originals
Pfaltzgraff

Enchanting Orchid
Nancy Prentiss

George & Martha
Nancy Prentiss

John & Priscilla
Nancy Prentiss

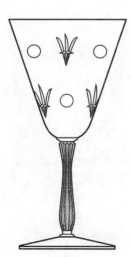

Lady Hilton
Nancy Prentiss

Milburn Rose
Nancy Prentiss

Bordeaux
Princess House

Esprit
Princess House

Fantasia
Princess House

Heritage
Princess House
aka "Princess Heritage"

Royal Highlights
Princess House

Queen's Lace
Queen Lace

RAC 1
Ransgil

Chantilly
Ransgil

Fuchsia
Ransgil

Kingsley
Ransgil

Rambling Rose
Ransgil
Gold Encrusted

Rhodora Rose
Ransgil

Silver Chalice
Ransgil

Knobby Bull's Eye
Red Cliff
Various Colors

Arbor
Reizart
270

Elegance
Reizart
270

Swirl
Reizart
270

Wheat
Reizart
270

American Beauty
Reizart
866

Geisha
Reizart
866

Marjory
Reizart
520

Arcadia
Reizart
933

Belvidere
Reizart
933

Nimbus
Reizart
933, Platinum Trim

Tuxedo
Reizart
933, Gold Trim

Lace
Reizart
1007, Platinum Trim

Malta
Reizart
771

Radiance
Reizart
784

Regency
Reizart
784

Vine
Reizart
784

Charnia
Reizart
854

Doria
Reizart
854

Flora
Reizart
854

Princess
Reizart
854

Sandra
Reizart
854

Brigitte
Reizart
6458

Lovelight
Reizart
6458

Contessa
Reizart
6447, Platinum Trim

Gold Rose
Reizart
6036, Gold Trim

June Rose
Reizart
6036

Platinum Rose
Reizart
6036, Platinum Trim

Classique
Reizart
1463

Green Mist
Reizart
1463, Green Bowl

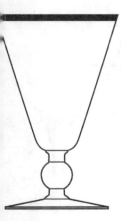

Brookmere
Reizart
997, Platinum Trim

Carmel
Reizart
997, Platinum Trim

997-1
Reizart
997, Gray Cut

Olympia
Reizart
997, Gold Trim

Nydia
Reizart
947, aka "Starlight"

Sonja
Reizart
947, Cube Stem

Kingsley
Reizart, Platinum
1008, "Princess," no trim

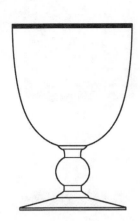

Encanto
Reizart
996, Platinum Trim

Miramar
Reizart
996, Platinum Trim

Sweetheart Rose
Reizart
996

Ingrid
Reizart
936

Wheat
Reizart
936

Coralbel
Reizart
968

Pine
Reizart
968

Roslyn
Reizart
968

Coronet
Reizart
1020

French Provincial
Reizart
1020, Gold Trim

Jewel
Reizart
1020, Platinum Trim

Tiara
Reizart
1020, Platinum Trim

Silhouette
Reizart
6027

Silver Twist
Reizart
6027, Platinum Trim

Antoinette
Reizart
6010

Millefleur
Reizart
6009

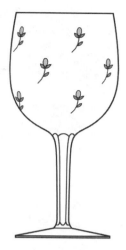

Rosepoint
Reizart
206

Falling Leaves
Reizart
986

Lily of the Valley
Reizart

Flair
Reizart

Bristol
Reizart

Lucerne
Reizart
7044

Queen Anne
Reizart
540

Steffens
Reizart

Monterey
Reizart
7160, Platinum Trim

Wyndcrest
Reizart
1101, Plain or with Platinum

Chesterfield
Rexxford

Solitaire
Rexxford

Strawberry Diamond
Rexxford

Anastasia
Reynolds

Bridal Veil
Reynolds
Platinum Trim

Midnight Halo
Reynolds
Black, Wine

Misty Rose
Reynolds
Pink

Royal Baroness
Reynolds
Gold or Platinum Trim

Sunnyvale
Reynolds

RDL 1
Riedel

RDL 2
Riedel

Amber Swirl
Riedel

Asymmetrico
Riedel

Blue Swirl
Riedel

Bruckner
Riedel
182

Bruxelles
Riedel
236

Carnival
Riedel

Chantilly
Riedel

Eva
Riedel
161

Exquisit
Riedel
103

Grand Prix
Riedel
119

Kongress
Riedel
241

Laudon Optic
Riedel
168

Lilac Swirl
Riedel

Monaco
Riedel
283

Montreal
Riedel
237

Nostalgia
Riedel
403

Pantheon
Riedel
333

Sommeliers
Riedel, 400
Wine Tasting: various shapes

Strauss
Riedel
181

York
Riedel
250/S100

Gallia
Rogaska

Rogaska

Country Garden
Rogaska

Jasmine
Rogaska

Queens
Rogaska

RGS 1
Rogaska

RGS 2
Rogaska

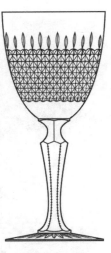

Chamberlin
Rogaska

Chatham
Rogaska
Also with Gold Trim

Eden
Rogaska

Ivy
Rogaska

Mariano
Rogaska
aka "Lyra"

Mayfair Gold
Rogaska

Raleigh
Rogaska
Gold Trim

Richmond
Rogaska
Also with Gold or Plat. Trim

Sheridan
Rogaska
Champagne Flute

RGS 3
Rogaska

Maymont
Rogaska

Palladio
Rogaska

Beauty
Rogaska
Iced Tea

Coronation
Rogaska
Also with Gold Trim

Covington
Rogaska
Newer, 6921/276

Memoir
Rogaska
Also with Gold Trim

Naples
Rogaska

Ellington
Rogaska

Juliet
Rogaska

Trilon
Rogaska

Vogue
Rogaska
Also with Gold Trim

Sundance
Rogaska

Tara Gold
Rogaska
Gold Trim

Chelsea
Rogaska

Galleria
Rogaska

Rogaska

Maestro
Rogaska

Raindrops
Rogaska

Soho
Rogaska

Ariel
Rogaska

Milan
Rogaska

Tuscany
Rogaska

Giselle
Rogaska

Swanlake
Rogaska

Aristocrat
Rogaska

Legend
Rogaska

Grace
Rogaska

Barrington
Rogaska
Also with Gold Trim

Saratoga
Rogaska
Gold Trim

Hamilton
Rogaska

Jefferson
Rogaska
Gold Trim

Marin
Rogaska
Brandy Glass

Cheers
Rogaska
Wine Tasting: various shapes

Covington
Rogaska
Older, 2921/276

Remembrance
Rogaska
Gold Trim and Ball

Tango
Rogaska

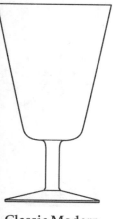

Classic Modern
Rosenthal
2000

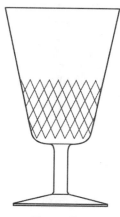

Cross Cut
Rosenthal
2000

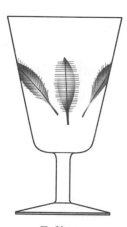

Foliage
Rosenthal
2000

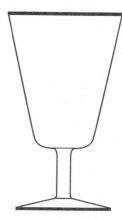

Gold Band
Rosenthal
2000

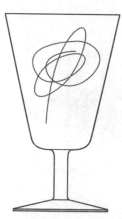

Goldaccord
Rosenthal
2000, Gold Design

Goldstrahlen
Rosenthal
2000, aka "Gloriana"

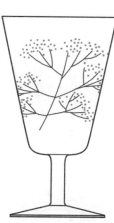

Goldzweig
Rosenthal
2000

Grasses
Rosenthal
2000

Parisian Spring
Rosenthal
2000

Platinum Band
Rosenthal
2000

Rosenthal

Quince
Rosenthal
2000

Shadow Rose
Rosenthal
2000

Spirale
Rosenthal
2000

2000-2
Rosenthal

2000-3
Rosenthal

Antoinette
Rosenthal
430

Ceres
Rosenthal
430

Fantasia
Rosenthal
430

Golden Palm
Rosenthal
430

Marshall Niel
Rosenthal
430

Moss Rose
Rosenthal
430

Orchid
Rosenthal
430

Pine Needles
Rosenthal
430

Regina
Rosenthal
430

Tropicana
Rosenthal
430

Wheat
Rosenthal
430

430-1
Rosenthal
Cut Rose

Arch
Rosenthal
Victoria Shape

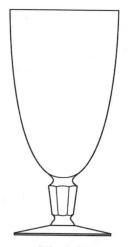

Victoria
Rosenthal

Summer Blossom
Rosenthal

RC 3
Rosenthal

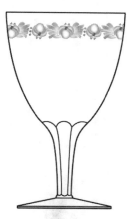

460-1
Rosenthal

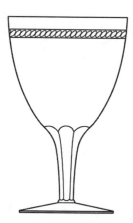

Claudia
Rosenthal
460, Cut 184

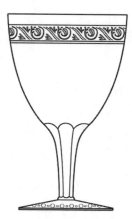

Duchess
Rosenthal
460, Etched

Parisian Spring
Rosenthal
460

Duo
Rosenthal
901

Spring
Rosenthal
901

Squares
Rosenthal
901

450-1
Rosenthal

English Karo
Rosenthal
450

Sanssouci
Rosenthal
450, aka "Baroque"

Saratoga
Rosenthal
450, aka "Facette"

Calice
Rosenthal
4100

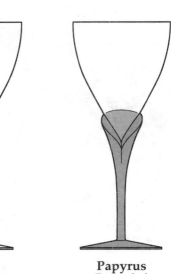

Papyrus
Rosenthal
4100, Green Stem

Fortuna
Rosenthal
Smoke Base

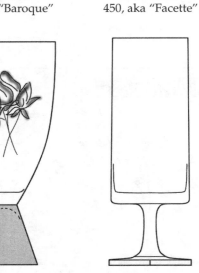

RC 8
Rosenthal
Smoke Base

Largo
Rosenthal
3200, Clear

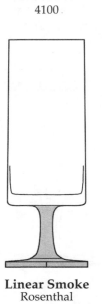

Linear Smoke
Rosenthal
3200, Smoke Base

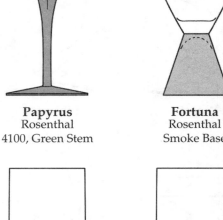

Linear Terzo
Rosenthal
3200, Cobalt Base

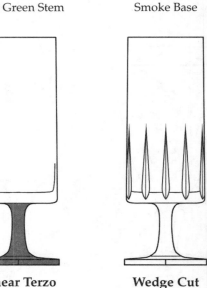

Wedge Cut
Rosenthal
3200, aka "Spearhead"

Romance I
Rosenthal
3003

Motif
Rosenthal
Romance 1 Stem

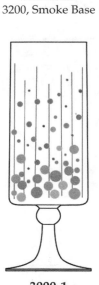
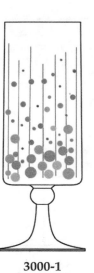

3000-1
Rosenthal
Bubbles

Variation
Rosenthal
2500, Smoke or Clear Stem

Variation
Rosenthal
2500, Cut Base

Motif
Rosenthal
Romance II Stem

Romance II
Rosenthal
3004

Romance Bouquet
Rosenthal
3004

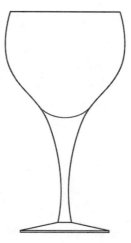

Lotus
Rosenthal
4000

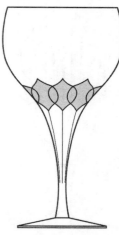

Lotus Blossoms
Rosenthal
4000

Lotus Cut
Rosenthal
4000, Clear or Blue

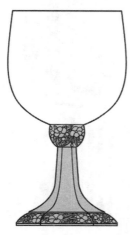

Elegance
Rosenthal
26040, Frosted Stem

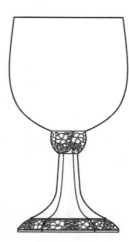

Maria
Rosenthal
6040

Catherine
Rosenthal
26050, Etched

Monbijou
Rosenthal
6050

Ophelia
Rosenthal
10377

American Rose
Rosenthal
377

RC 1
Rosenthal
Twisted Foot

Geisha
Rosenthal

Tulip
Rosenthal
700

Rosenthal

Tulip Rays
Rosenthal
700

Ultra
Rosenthal
4300, Blue Streaks

Fuga
Rosenthal
608

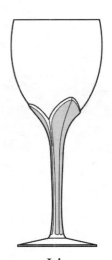

Iris
Rosenthal
Clear or Frosted Stem

Asymmetria
Rosenthal
0388

Century
Rosenthal
295

Clairon
Rosenthal
0900

Blanc de Blanc
Rosenthal
0373

Magic Flute
Rosenthal
Gold Design

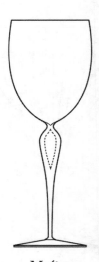

Maítre
Rosenthal
304

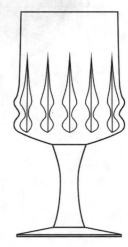

Holdfast
Rosenthal
513

Bacchus
Rosenthal
514

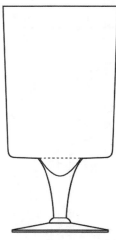

Composition "G"
Rosenthal
101

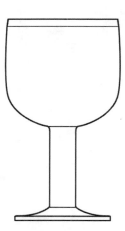

Cordon
Rosenthal
0222

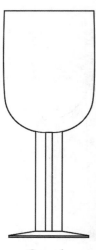

Cupola
Rosenthal
6150

Motif
Rosenthal
Regina Shape

RC 4
Rosenthal

RC 5
Rosenthal
White Stem

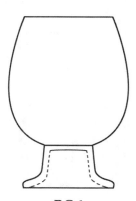

RC 6
Rosenthal
Studio Line

Plus
Rosenthal
9100

Polaris
Rosenthal
520, Cut

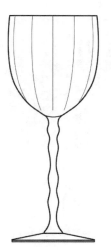

Polygon
Rosenthal
0346

Samara
Rosenthal
5200

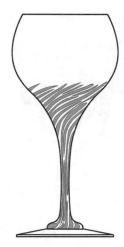

Snowflower
Rosenthal
4200, aka "Edelweiss"

Soiree
Rosenthal
440

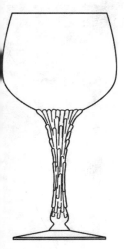

Split
Rosenthal
9600

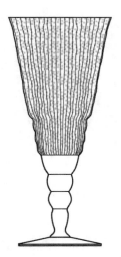

Structure
Rosenthal
395

Patricia
Rosenthal
10 Cuts on Base

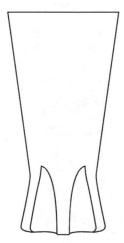

Patricia
Rosenthal
5 Cuts on Base

Schleirglass
Rosenthal
0335

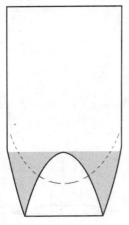

Skal
Rosenthal
6300/0004

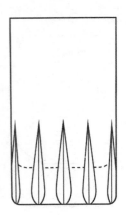

Tivoli
Rosenthal
5100

RBC 1
Royal Benton
Yellow

RBR 1
Royal Brierley

Ascot
Royal Brierley
2690

Eton
Royal Brierley
3204

Plymouth
Royal Brierley

Regent
Royal Brierley
C1309

Stirling
Royal Brierley
3551

Warwick
Royal Brierley

Bruce
Royal Brierley
1463

Bruce
Royal Brierley
3549

Goodwood
Royal Brierley
C3285

Cornflower
Royal Brierley
4224

Braemar
Royal Brierley
4998, Tall Stem

Coventry
Royal Brierley
2781

Honeysuckle
Royal Brierley
3527

Kendall
Royal Brierley
C3205

Lady Brierley
Royal Brierley

Princess Charming
Royal Brierley
D625

Gainsborough
Royal Brierley
2687

Dorchester
Royal Brierley
C2685

Marlborough
Royal Brierley
C2689

Stratford
Royal Brierley

Windsor
Royal Brierley

Rose
Royal Brierley
C677

Westminster
Royal Brierley

Winchester
Royal Brierley
C312

Braemar
Royal Brierley
2148, Short Stem

Tiger Lily
Royal Brierley
5120

Fuchsia
Royal Brierley
3873

York
Royal Brierley
5084

Elizabeth
Royal Brierley
1650

Hibiscus
Royal Brierley

RCY 1
Royal Crystal Rock

Ambassador
Royal Crystal Rock

Aurea
Royal Crystal Rock
Also with Gold Trim

Columbia
Royal Crystal Rock

Edelweiss
Royal Crystal Rock

Gala
Royal Crystal Rock
High Ball

Gemini/Edelweiss
Royal Crystal Rock

Helen
Royal Crystal Rock

Laurie
Royal Crystal Rock

Linea
Royal Crystal Rock

Linea Gala
Royal Crystal Rock

London
Royal Crystal Rock

Magnolia
Royal Crystal Rock
"Prima Vera" Line

Opera
Royal Crystal Rock

Palace
Royal Crystal Rock

Shannon
Royal Crystal Rock

Angelique
Royal Doulton

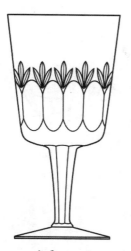

Ashmont
Royal Doulton

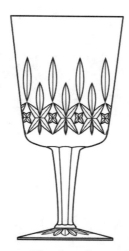

Sherbrooke
Royal Doulton

Rondelay
Royal Doulton

Sonnet
Royal Doulton

Belvedere
Royal Doulton

Clarendon
Royal Doulton

Rochelle
Royal Doulton

Balmoral
Royal Doulton

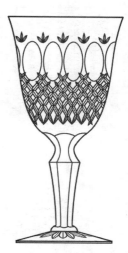

Windsor
Royal Doulton

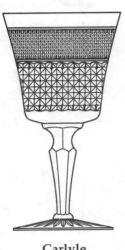

Carlyle
Royal Doulton

Vanborough
Royal Doulton

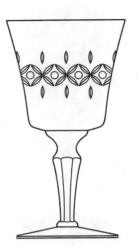

Mirabeau
Royal Doulton

Arden
Royal Doulton

Ascot
Royal Doulton
Also with Gold Trim

Stratford
Royal Doulton

Summit
Royal Doulton

Amanda
Royal Doulton

Aria
Royal Doulton

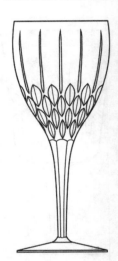

Destiny
Royal Doulton

Hampstead
Royal Doulton

Kensington
Royal Doulton

Knightsbridge
Royal Doulton

Westminster
Royal Doulton

Lisa
Royal Doulton

Mayfair
Royal Doulton

Diana
Royal Doulton

Athena
Royal Doulton

Janet
Royal Doulton

Jillian
Royal Doulton

Wellesley
Royal Doulton
Also with Gold Trim

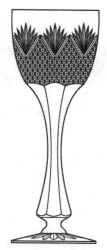

Queen's Park
Royal Doulton

Gallerie
Royal Doulton

Clifton
Royal Doulton

Prince Charles
Royal Doulton
Gin & Tonic

Juno
Royal Doulton

Georgian
Royal Doulton

Prince Regent
Royal Doulton

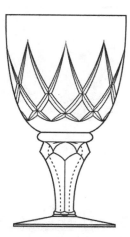

Alycia
Royal Leerdam

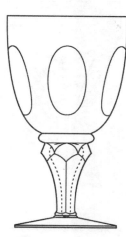

Juliana
Royal Leerdam
aka "Queen Juliana"

Princess Astrid
Royal Leerdam

Regal
Royal Leerdam

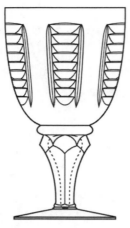

Rembrandt
Royal Leerdam

RLE 2
Royal Leerdam

Rondo
Royal Leerdam

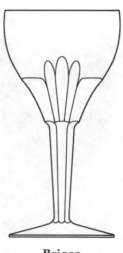

Brioso
Royal Leerdam

Carola
Royal Leerdam

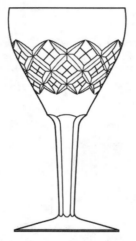

Eugenia
Royal Leerdam

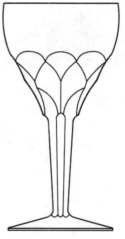

Gloria
Royal Leerdam

Lyra
Royal Leerdam

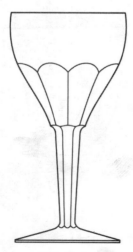

Victoria
Royal Leerdam

Rubato
Royal Leerdam

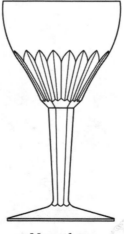

Nymphea
Royal Leerdam

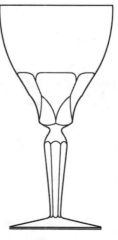

Canto
Royal Leerdam

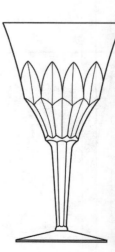

Contessa
Royal Leerdam

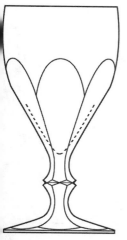

Boccale
Royal Leerdam

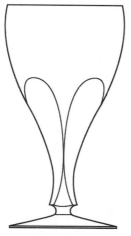

Capriole
Royal Leerdam

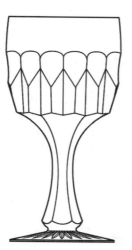

Ambassador
Royal Leerdam

Netherlands
Royal Leerdam

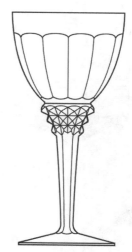

Starlight
Royal Leerdam

Romance
Royal Leerdam

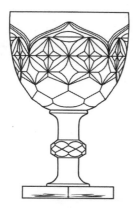

Alhambra
Royal Leerdam

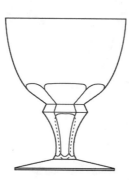

Bernina
Royal Leerdam

Elegance
Royal Leerdam

Royalty
Royal Leerdam

Tiara
Royal Leerdam

Van Dijck
Royal Leerdam

Debutante
Royal Leerdam

Gothic
Royal Leerdam

RLE 6
Royal Leerdam

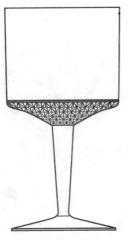

Marquise
Royal Leerdam

Air-Twist
Royal Leerdam
Williamsburg Reproduction

Baluster
Royal Leerdam
Williamsburg Reproduction

Bamboo
Royal Leerdam

Simplicity
Royal Leerdam

Gilde
Royal Leerdam

Regal Gilde
Royal Leerdam

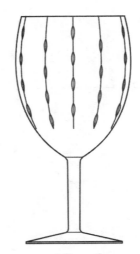

Allegro
Royal Leerdam

Tango
Royal Leerdam
Clear or Smoke

Ceres
Royal Leerdam

Black Tulip
Royal Leerdam
Smoke Colored

Daphne
Royal Leerdam
Clear or Smoke

Radiance
Royal Leerdam

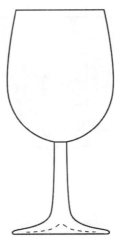

Simplicity
Royal Leerdam
aka "Prelude"

Empress
Royal Moselle
Iridescent

Encore
Royal Moselle
Sterling Trim

Harvest
Royal Moselle

Rambler Rose
Royal Moselle

Rosine
Royal Moselle

Serene
Royal Moselle

RPC 1
Royal Prestige
Black

Alto
Royal Worcester

Fantasy
Royal Worcester
Platinum Trim

Hanover
Royal Worcester

Moonlight
Royal Worcester

Nassau
Royal Worcester

Navarre
Royal Worcester
Clear or Smoke

Prelude
Royal Worcester

Radiance
Royal Worcester
Gold Trim

Rhine
Royal Worcester

SAS 1
Sasaki
Pink Bowl and Stem

SAS 2
Sasaki

SAS 3
Sasaki
Platinum

SAS 4
Sasaki
Light Blue

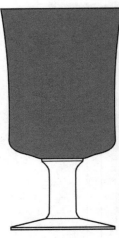

SAS 5
Sasaki
Cobalt Bowl

Aegean
Sasaki
Various Colors

Andoas
Sasaki

Astro
Sasaki
Clear or Blue

Bamboo
Sasaki

Belinda
Sasaki
Various Colors

Bisanzio
Sasaki
Clear or Violet

Black Tie
Sasaki

Candace
Sasaki

Capistrano
Sasaki
Various Colors

Cathadia
Sasaki
Amber Stem, Green Bas

Charade
Sasaki
osted Stem, Gold Accents

Chicago
Sasaki
Gold or Amethyst Accents

Classico
Sasaki

Concorde
Sasaki

Coronation
Sasaki
Various Colors

Double Helix
Sasaki

Eclipse
Sasaki
Wine

Ellessee
Sasaki

Engagement
Sasaki
Gold Band

Eon
Sasaki
Various Colors

Grand Hawthorne
Sasaki
Various Colors

Hampton
Sasaki
Various Colors

Hana
Sasaki
Frosted Stem

Harmony
Sasaki
Various Colors

Hawthorne
Sasaki
Various Colors

Hilton
Sasaki
Various Colors

Isabelle
Sasaki
Frosted Ball

Jomon
Sasaki
Frosted Stem

Kahala
Sasaki
Frosted Stem

Laurel
Sasaki
Clear or Frosted Green Ste

Lightning
Sasaki
Clear or with Black Stem

Lily of the Valley
Sasaki
Clear or Frosted Stem

Lotus
Sasaki

Lumina
Sasaki
Various Colors

Luxembourg
Sasaki

Malibu
Sasaki
Black Stem, Champ. Flute

Mariya
Sasaki
Various Colors

Marly
Sasaki

Marquisa
Sasaki

Metropolis
Sasaki

Midsummer
Sasaki

Normandy
Sasaki

Omnia
Sasaki
Gold or Gold & Blk. Rings

Orbit
Sasaki
Frosted or Gold Accents

Plein Jour
Sasaki

Princess
Sasaki
ME905

Printemps
Sasaki
Clear or Pink

Prism
Sasaki

Rapture
Sasaki
Various Colors

Reflections
Sasaki
Various Colors

Regency
Sasaki
Frosted Stem

Renaissance
Sasaki
Gold or Platinum Trim

Royale
Sasaki
Black Stem

San Marino
Sasaki
Blue Ball, Black Foot

Sergio
Sasaki
Black Stem

Seville
Sasaki

Silk
Sasaki

Sorbet
Sasaki
Green Frosted Stem

Statue of Liberty
Sasaki
Champagne Flute

Stone
Sasaki
Stone Base

Suninke
Sasaki
Colored Stems

Swizzle
Sasaki
Clear or Black Stem

Tucano
Sasaki, Black or Frosted
Stem, Gold Accents

Tulipe
Sasaki
Various Colors

Veronique
Sasaki

Versailles
Sasaki
Clear or Green

Wheat
Sasaki

Windows
Sasaki

Wings
Sasaki

Daffodil
Schmid

Tulip
Schmid

Garda
F. Schmidt
Amber, Green, or Rose

Platinum Sovereign
Schneegattern Glass

Aegean
Schott-Zwiesel

Ceremony
Schott-Zwiesel

Chantilly
Schott-Zwiesel
Also with Gold Trim

Concord
Schott-Zwiesel
Gold Trim

SCZ 3
Schott-Zwiesel

Carlton
Schott-Zwiesel
Gold or Platinum Trim

Classic
Schott-Zwiesel

Clifton
Schott-Zwiesel

Fairmont
Schott-Zwiesel

Excellence
Schott-Zwiesel

Pageant
Schott-Zwiesel
Platinum Trim

Premier
Schott-Zwiesel
Gold Trim

Prestige
Schott-Zwiesel

Avenue
Schott-Zwiesel

Tudor
Schott-Zwiesel

SCZ 4
Schott-Zwiesel
"Christinenhutte"

Adagio
Schott-Zwiesel

Almeria
Schott-Zwiesel

Mykonos
Schott-Zwiesel
Gold Trim

Christine
Schott-Zwiesel
Wine

Antoinette
Schott-Zwiesel

Desiree
Schott-Zwiesel

Silver Jubilee
Schott-Zwiesel
Platinum Trim

Senorita
Schott-Zwiesel

President
Schott-Zwiesel

Delilah
Schott-Zwiesel

Diana
Schott-Zwiesel

Doreen
Schott-Zwiesel

Verve
Schott-Zwiesel

Celebration
Schott-Zwiesel

Wessex
Schott-Zwiesel

Wessex Gold
Schott-Zwiesel
Gold Trim

Concerto
Schott-Zwiesel

Suite
Schott-Zwiesel

Linda
Schott-Zwiesel

Mayfair
Schott-Zwiesel

Tiffany
Schott-Zwiesel

Westminster
Schott-Zwiesel

Volterra
Schott-Zwiesel

SCZ 2
Schott-Zwiesel

Contour
Schott-Zwiesel

Gardone
Schott-Zwiesel

Schott-Zwiesel

Flamenco
Schott-Zwiesel

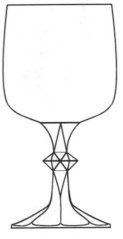

Melodia
Schott-Zwiesel

Tango
Schott-Zwiesel

Tarantella
Schott-Zwiesel

Pirouette
Schott-Zwiesel

Gala
Schott-Zwiesel
aka "Arabesque"

Revue
Schott-Zwiesel
Also with Gold Trim

Starlyte
Schott-Zwiesel
Also with Gold Trim

Royale
Schott-Zwiesel

Duet
Schott-Zwiesel

Bonheur
Schott-Zwiesel

Fortune
Schott-Zwiesel

Feria
Schott-Zwiesel

Finesse
Schott-Zwiesel
aka "Finesse Deluxe"

Richmond
Schott-Zwiesel

Banquet
Schott-Zwiesel

Neckar
Schott-Zwiesel
Clear or Smoke

Neckar
Schott-Zwiesel
Gold or Platinum Trim

Europa
Schott-Zwiesel
Clear, Pink, or Smoke

Europa
Schott-Zwiesel
Gold or Plat. Band

Meran
Schott-Zwiesel
ear, Smoke, or with Plat. Trim

Buffet
Schott-Zwiesel

Hexagon
Schott-Zwiesel
Black Thread in Stem

Cabernet
Schott-Zwiesel

Cinderella
Schott-Zwiesel

Henriette
Schott-Zwiesel

Columbia
Schott-Zwiesel

Excelsior
Schott-Zwiesel
aka "Edition Deluxe"

Auberge
Schott-Zwiesel

Aura
Schott-Zwiesel

Imperial
Schott-Zwiesel

Selection
Schott-Zwiesel

Conte
Schott-Zwiesel
Various Colors

Josephine
Schott-Zwiesel

Eclair
Schott-Zwiesel
Clear or Turquoise

Florida
Schott-Zwiesel

Ballet
Schott-Zwiesel

Pasodoble
Schott-Zwiesel
Frosted Accents

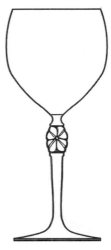

Viva
Schott-Zwiesel

Viva Satin
Schott-Zwiesel

Camelot
Schott-Zwiesel
Various Stem Accents

Noblesse
Schott-Zwiesel

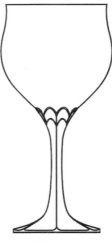

Musica
Schott-Zwiesel

Lars
Schott-Zwiesel

Ovation
Schott-Zwiesel

Pamela
Schott-Zwiesel

Vogue
Schott-Zwiesel
Turquoise Stem

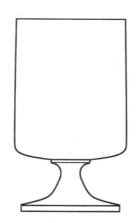

Roma
Schott-Zwiesel

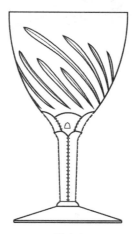

331-1
Seneca

388-5
Seneca

484-5
Seneca

485-3
Seneca

515-5
Seneca

913-3
Seneca

913-4
Seneca

1235-1
Seneca

1258 ½-2
Seneca

Asteric
Seneca
578, Cut 1377

Cut 369
Seneca
515

Cut 1009
Seneca
912

Cut 1009
Seneca
913

Decoration 501
Seneca, 993
Gold inside bowl

Decoration 502
Seneca, 993
Gold not inside bowl

Decoration 503
Seneca
993, Gold Inlay and Trim

By Candlelight
Sevron
Made for Home Decorators

Garden Queen
Sevron

Moonglow
Sevron

Starfire
Sevron

Celebrity
Shelbourne
Pink

Bridal Lace
Silver City
Sterling Decoration

SIN 1
Sinclair

Kungsholm
Skruf

Stockholm
Skruf

Moon & Star
Smith Glass
Various Colors

Sculptura II
Smith Glass
Various Colors

Royal Platinum
Society, Platinum
Brandy Glass

Royal Splendor
Society

Provence
Sophienthal

Aida
Spiegelau

Fedora
Spiegelau
Optic

Helena
Spiegelau

Luna
Spiegelau
Gold Trim

Mignon
Spiegelau

Tosca
Spiegelau

Undine
Spiegelau

SPI 1
Spiegelau

Bargello
Spiegelau

Louvre
Spiegelau
Gold Trim

Prado
Spiegelau
Gold or Platinum Trim

Metropolitan
Spiegelau
60235

Eremitage
Spiegelau

Anemone
Spiegelau

Begonia
Spiegelau

Lilium
Spiegelau

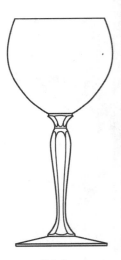

Malva
Spiegelau

Narcissus
Spiegelau

Vesta
Spiegelau

Crescendo
Spiegelau

Rondino
Spiegelau

Raphaela
Spiegelau

Tamara
Spiegelau

Tradition
Spiegelau
910

Miami
Spiegelau

Toselli
Spiegelau

Belvedere
Spiegelau

Boticelli
Spiegelau
Gold Accent

Venus
Spiegelau

Champs Élysées
Spiegelau

Park Lane
Spiegelau
Gold or Platinum Trim

Via Veneto
Spiegelau

Ponte Vecchio
Spiegelau

Pretiosa
Spiegelau

Donizetti
Spiegelau

Festival
Spiegelau

Fontaine
Spiegelau

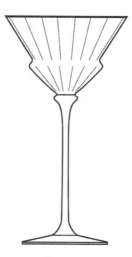

Giselle
Spiegelau

Tiara
Spiegelau

Twist
Spiegelau

Sereno
Spiegelau
230-E, Gold Trim

Paola
Spiegelau

Spiegelau, Spode

Arkade
Spiegelau

Aria
Spode

Cardinal
Spode

Carillon
Spode

Catherine
Spode

Christine
Spode

Concerto
Spode

Constance
Spode

Intermezzo
Spode

Jennifer
Spode

Joanne
Spode

Karen
Spode

Maureen
Spode

Patricia
Spode

Prelude
Spode

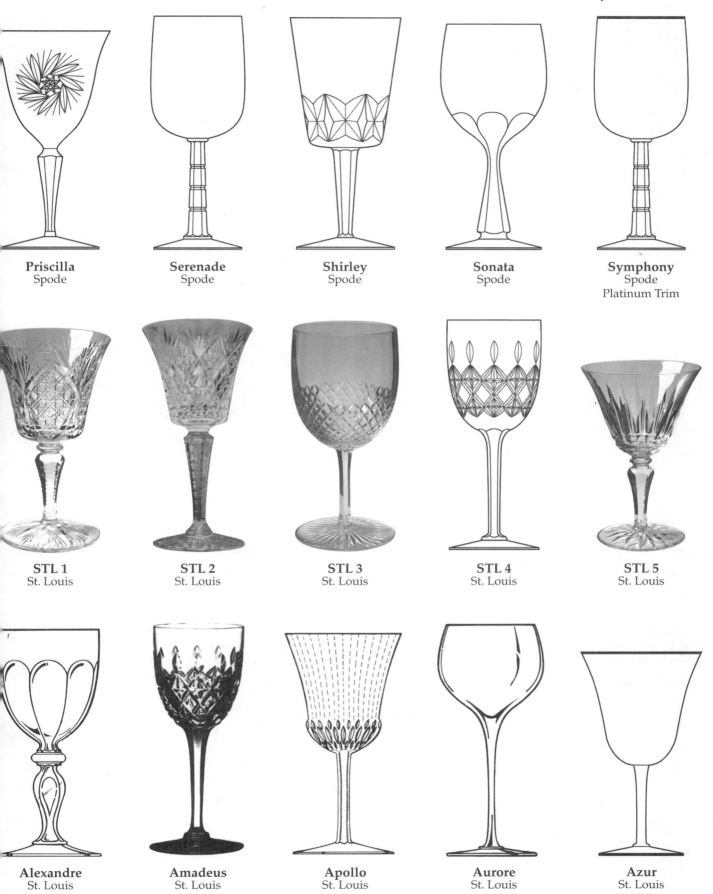

Priscilla
Spode

Serenade
Spode

Shirley
Spode

Sonata
Spode

Symphony
Spode
Platinum Trim

STL 1
St. Louis

STL 2
St. Louis

STL 3
St. Louis

STL 4
St. Louis

STL 5
St. Louis

Alexandre
St. Louis
Also with Gold Trim

Amadeus
St. Louis

Apollo
St. Louis
Also with Gold Trim

Aurore
St. Louis

Azur
St. Louis
Gold Trim

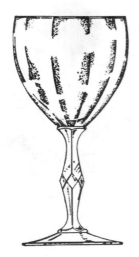

Bartholdi
St. Louis
Also with Gold Trim

Bartholdi
St. Louis
Etched, Gold Inlay

Bizet
St. Louis
Also with Gold Trim

Bristol
St. Louis

Bubbles
St. Louis
Also with Gold Trim

Camargue
St. Louis

Cerdagne
St. Louis
Also with Gold Trim

Chambord
St. Louis

Chantilly
St. Louis

Cleo
St. Louis

Congress
St. Louis

Daphne
St. Louis

Diamant
St. Louis

Excellence
St. Louis
Gold Trim

Faust
St. Louis

Firmament
St. Louis
Blue Bowl, Gold Trim

Florence
St. Louis
Plain or Cased with Gold

Fontainebleau
St. Louis

Grand Lieu
St. Louis

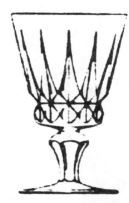

Guernesey
St. Louis

Jersey
St. Louis

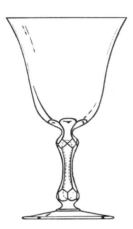

Lozere
St. Louis
Also with Gold Trim

Massenet
St. Louis

Massenet
St. Louis
Etched with Gold Inlay

Messine
St. Louis

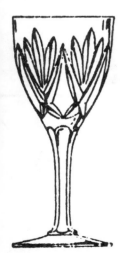

Monaco
St. Louis

Orleans
St. Louis

Pline
St. Louis

Pomerol
St. Louis

Provence
St. Louis

Renaissance
St. Louis
Various Colors

Rodin
St. Louis

Stella
St. Louis
Gold Encrusted

Tacite
St. Louis

Tarn
St. Louis

Thistle
St. Louis
Gold Encrusted

Tommy
St. Louis
Clear or Cased Colors

Trevi
St. Louis

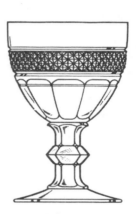

Trianon
St. Louis

Trianon
St. Louis
Etched with Gold Inlay

Virginia
St. Louis

STI 1
Sterling

SP443
Steuben

6268
Steuben

7666
Steuben

7725
Steuben

7737
Steuben

7846
Steuben

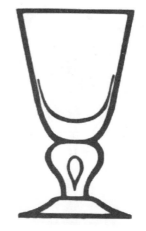

7877
Steuben

7917
Steuben
Liquor Cocktail

7924
Steuben

7925
Steuben

7926
Steuben

8011
Steuben

Georgian
Steuben
7725

Bavarian Countess
Stonegate

Harvest Stars
Stonegate

Midnight Rose
Stonegate

Princess
Stonegate

Spring Breeze
Stonegate

Wooddale
Stonegate

Ellesmere
Stuart

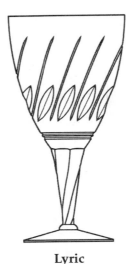

Lyric
Stuart

Coronation
Stuart

St. James
Stuart

Windermere
Stuart

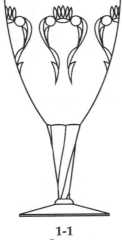

1-1
Stuart

1-3
Stuart

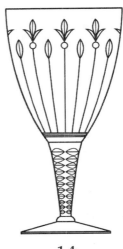

1-4
Stuart

Ariel
Stuart

Rhythm
Stuart

Westbury
Stuart

Alexandra
Stuart
Gold Encrusted

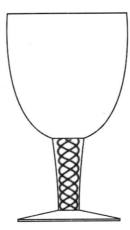

Sonata
Stuart

14-1
Stuart

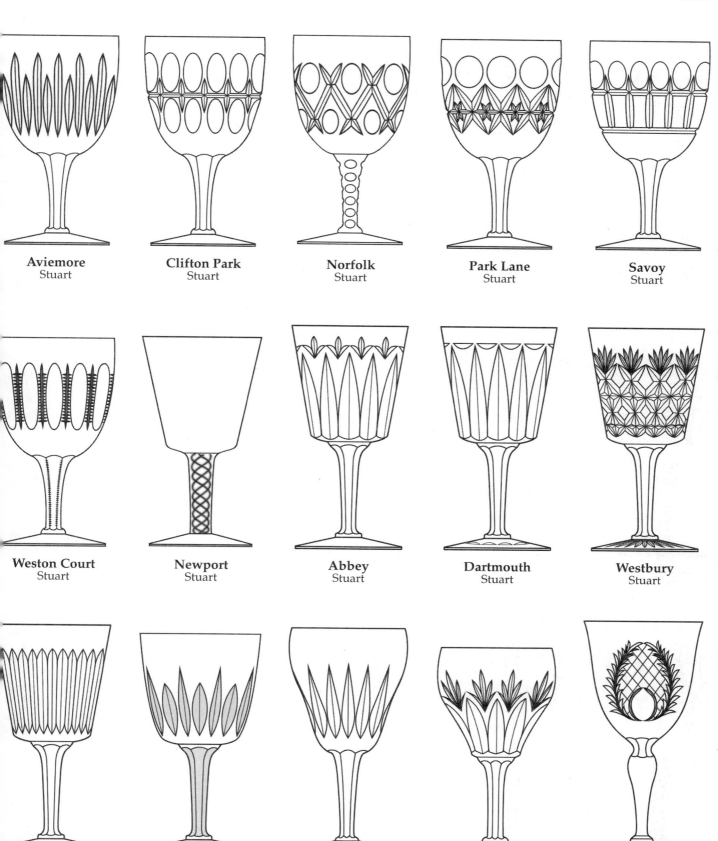

Aviemore
Stuart

Clifton Park
Stuart

Norfolk
Stuart

Park Lane
Stuart

Savoy
Stuart

Weston Court
Stuart

Newport
Stuart

Abbey
Stuart

Dartmouth
Stuart

Westbury
Stuart

21-1
Stuart

Versailles
Stuart
Gray Cutting and Stem

Claridge
Stuart

Cardinal
Stuart

Amherst
Stuart

Aragon
Stuart

Camelot
Stuart

Empire
Stuart

Marlborough
Stuart

Hardwicke
Stuart

Victoria
Stuart
Gold Trim

Canterbury
Stuart

Georgian
Stuart

Knightsbridge
Stuart

Edwardian
Stuart

Tintern
Stuart

York
Stuart

36-1
Stuart

Braemar
Stuart

Hampshire
Stuart

Minuet
Stuart

Regent
Stuart

Chippendale
Stuart

Dorset
Stuart

43-1
Stuart

Montrose
Stuart

Winchester
Stuart
Sherry

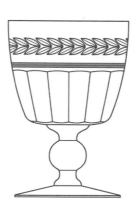

Arundel
Stuart

Imperial
Stuart

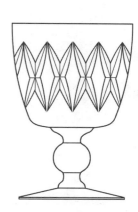

Lovat
Stuart

Ludlow
Stuart

Beaconsfield
Stuart
Ball Stem

Cathedral
Stuart

Darlington
Stuart

Victoria
Stuart
Ball Stem

Ashford
Stuart

Glengarry
Stuart

Mansfield
Stuart

Cheltenham
Stuart

Dunkeld
Stuart

Glendevon
Stuart

Richmond
Stuart

Monarch
Stuart
Gold Encrusted

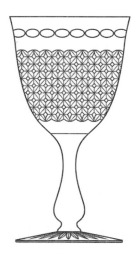

Catherine
Stuart

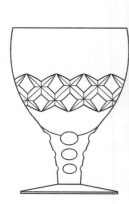

Beau
Stuart

Carlingford
Stuart

Medley
Stuart

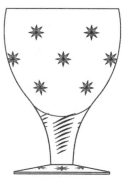

Startime
Stuart

Woodchester
Stuart

Concerto
Stuart

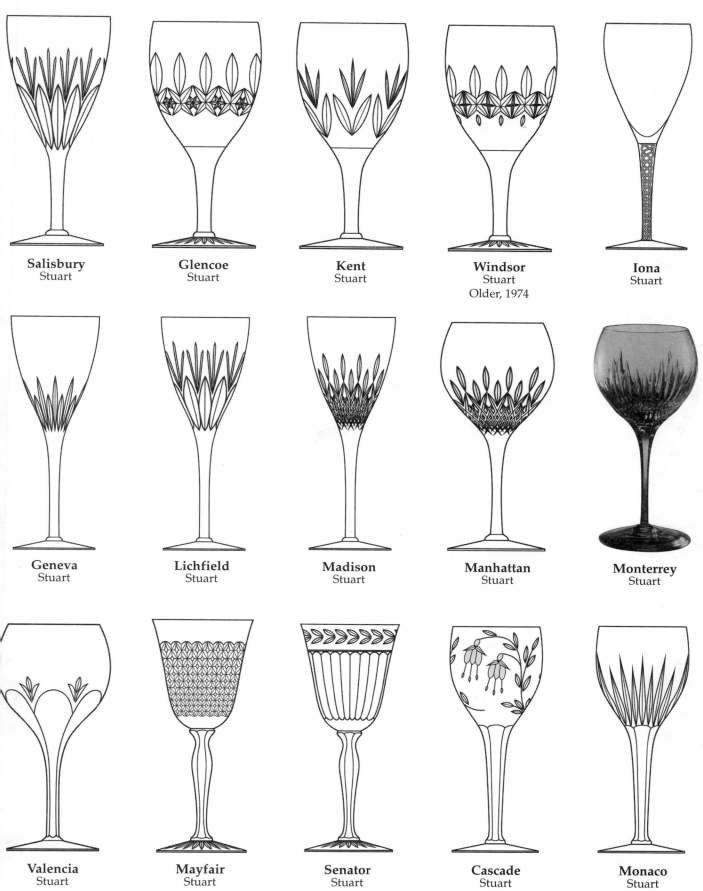

Salisbury
Stuart

Glencoe
Stuart

Kent
Stuart

Windsor
Stuart
Older, 1974

Iona
Stuart

Geneva
Stuart

Lichfield
Stuart

Madison
Stuart

Manhattan
Stuart

Monterrey
Stuart

Valencia
Stuart

Mayfair
Stuart

Senator
Stuart

Cascade
Stuart

Monaco
Stuart

Shaftesbury
Stuart

Eden
Stuart

Oleta
Stuart

St. George
Stuart

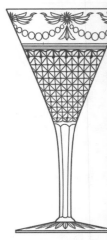

Beaconsfield
Stuart
Straight Stem

Medici
Stuart

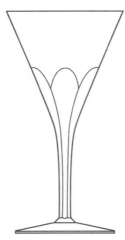

Symphony
Stuart

Harlech
Stuart

Anastasia
Stuart
Gold Inlay

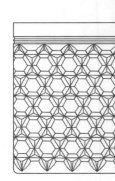

Hobnail
Stuart

Kingsley
Susquehanna

SUS 4
Susquehanna

56-1
Susquehanna

Celeste
Susquehanna
56

Fantasy
Susquehanna
56

Fascination
Susquehanna
56

Coronet
Susquehanna
S200

Fair Lady
Susquehanna
S200, Platinum Trim

Tiara
Susquehanna
S200, Platinum Trim

Echo
Susquehanna
4151

Six Point Star
Susquehanna
4151

Wreath
Susquehanna
4151

Celeste
Susquehanna
42

Fascination
Susquehanna
42

Milton
Susquehanna
42

Prairie
Susquehanna
42

Six Point Star
Susquehanna
42

Wood Violet
Susquehanna
42

Minerva
Susquehanna
24 TS

SUS 1
Susquehanna

Susquehanna

SUS 3
Susquehanna

Fascination
Susquehanna
R20

Bridal Bouquet
Susquehanna
425

Gold Dawn
Susquehanna
425, Gold Trim

Golden Mist
Susquehanna
425, Gold Encrusted

Majestic
Susquehanna
425, Gold Trim

Silver Dawn
Susquehanna
425, Platinum Trim

Simplicity
Susquehanna
425, Platinum Trim

SUS 2
Susquehanna

Rhapsody
Susquehanna
3848

Salina
Susquehanna
3848

Larraine
Susquehanna
230, Platinum Trim

Salem
Susquehanna
230

Silver Wheat
Susquehanna
61

Crescendo
Susquehanna
Iced Tea

Wood Violet
Susquehanna
Wine

Elegance
Sussmuth

Nassau
Sussmuth
Smoke

Navarre
Sussmuth
Clear or Smoke

Tyrol
Sussmuth

Albian
Swedish

Elinor
Swedish

Astrid
Swedish
5 Lobe Stem

Gulli
Swedish, 4 Lobe Stem
Clear, Blue, Gold, or Smoke

North Star
Swedish

Sigrid
Swedish
Amber

Brookdale
Justin Tharaud

Chanson
Justin Tharaud

Chantilly
Justin Tharaud

Embassy
Justin Tharaud

Monoco
Justin Tharaud
Various Colors

President
Justin Tharaud
Various Colors, Gold Encr.

Royal Peacock
Justin Tharaud

Bernadotte Minton
Theresienthal
Gold Encrusted

Connaisseur Minton
Theresienthal
Gold Encrusted

Gloria
Theresienthal

Hyde Park
Theresienthal
Brown

Madrid
Theresienthal

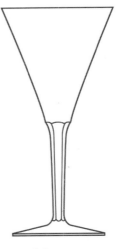

Musette
Theresienthal

TMC 1
Thomas

Colonna
Thomas

Colonna Graphic
Thomas

Coppa
Thomas

Corda
Thomas

Holiday
Thomas

Impala
Thomas

Tivoli
Thomas

Trend
Thomas

Ponderosa Pine
Tiara

TIF 1
Tiffin

TIF 2
Tiffin

TIF 3
Tiffin

TIF 5
Tiffin

TIF 6
Tiffin

TIF 4
Tiffin

2000-3
Tiffin

Coronet
Tiffin
2822

NE 259
Tiffin
14196, Needle Etching

Special Minton
Tiffin
14196, Gold Encrusted

Gothic
Tiffin
14199, Gold Encrusted

Psyche
Tiffin
15003, Green Trim

15003-1
Tiffin
Brown Accent

15022-1
Tiffin
Green Accent

15024-1
Tiffin
Rose colored

Cut 436
Tiffin
15024

15032-1
Tiffin
Rose colored

15042-3
Tiffin
Gold Encrusted

Cordelia
Tiffin
15048, Mandarin

15065-1
Tiffin
Mandarin

15067-2
Tiffin

15067-3
Tiffin

15070-2
Tiffin

15071-1
Tiffin

15072-3
Tiffin

15073-3
Tiffin

15073-4
Tiffin

15074-5
Tiffin

15074-6
Tiffin
Sherbet

15082-3
Tiffin

15083-1
Tiffin

15088-2
Tiffin

17323-1
Tiffin

17323-2
Tiffin

17348-5
Tiffin

17361-2
Tiffin

17371-1
Tiffin

Mystic
Tiffin
17372

Lenox
Tiffin
17378, Gold Inlay & Trim

Lenox Wheat
Tiffin
17391

17492-2
Tiffin

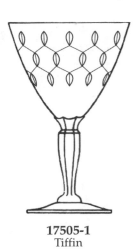

17505-1
Tiffin

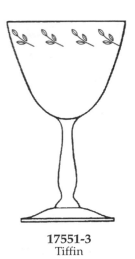

17551-3
Tiffin

Princess Rose
Tiffin
17566, Platinum or Plain

17566-3
Tiffin

Blue Seranada
Tiffin
17574, Blue Bowl

Granada
Tiffin
17593, Bubble in Stem

17594-13
Tiffin

Lenox Elmwood
Tiffin
17596, Gold Inlay

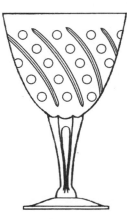

17596-2
Tiffin
Bubble in Stem

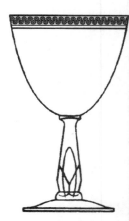

Finale
Tiffin, 17614, Platinum
Made for American Mano

17623-5
Tiffin
Bubble in Stem

Starfire
Tiffin
17634, Formerly 17634-1

Seventeen
Tiffin
17638, Bubble in Stem

Engagement
Tiffin
17648, Gold Trim

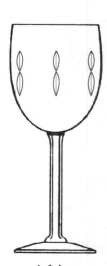

Adrian
Tiffin
17662

17664-2
Tiffin

Berkeley
Tipperary (Stefan Line)
1300/158

Cathedral
Tipperary (Stefan Line)
1300/101

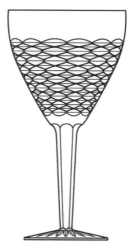

Cricklewood
Tipperary (Stefan Line)
1808/144

Dove Hill
Tipperary
Wine

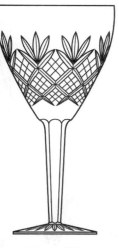

Granville
Tipperary (Stefan Line)
1808/135

Shannon
Tipperary (Stefan Line)
1300/105

Slievenamon
Tipperary

St. Stephen's
Tipperary (Stefan Line)
1300/120

TOY 1
Toscany

Ariel
Toscany

Augusta
Toscany

Ballerina
Toscany

Clipper
Toscany

Debbie
Toscany

Empress
Toscany

Heather/Iris
Toscany

Iris
Toscany

Iris Lustre
Toscany
Iridescent Bowl

Lillian
Toscany

Metropolis
Toscany

Muirfield
Toscany

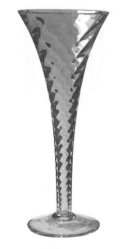

Perignon
Toscany
Champ. Flute Only

Queen's Lustreware
Toscany
Platinum Coating

Sierra
Toscany

Spectrum
Toscany

Sutton
Toscany

Symphony
Toscany

Twinkle
Toscany

Virna
Toscany

Wheat
Toscany

Yale
Toscany

Candlelight
Towle

King Richard
Towle

Tudor
Towle

Tudor Gold
Towle
Gold Trim

Leyland
Towle

Serenade
Towle

Silhouette
Towle

Cornet
Towle

Reflections
Towle

Riviera
Towle

Essex
Towle

Majesty
Towle

Marquis
Towle

307

Tiara
Towle

Antique Satin
Towle
Frosted Stem

Ardmore
Towle (Optic)
Champagne Flute

Fanfare
Towle
Champagne Flute

Fantasy
Towle

Kirkland
Towle

York
Towle
Optic

Halifax
Towle

Manchester
Towle
Optic

Westerly
Towle
Optic

Windham
Towle

Belvedere
Traunkristall (Austria)

TRH 1
Treasure House Crystal

Burleigh
Tudor
Cut Ball Stem

Holbein
Tudor

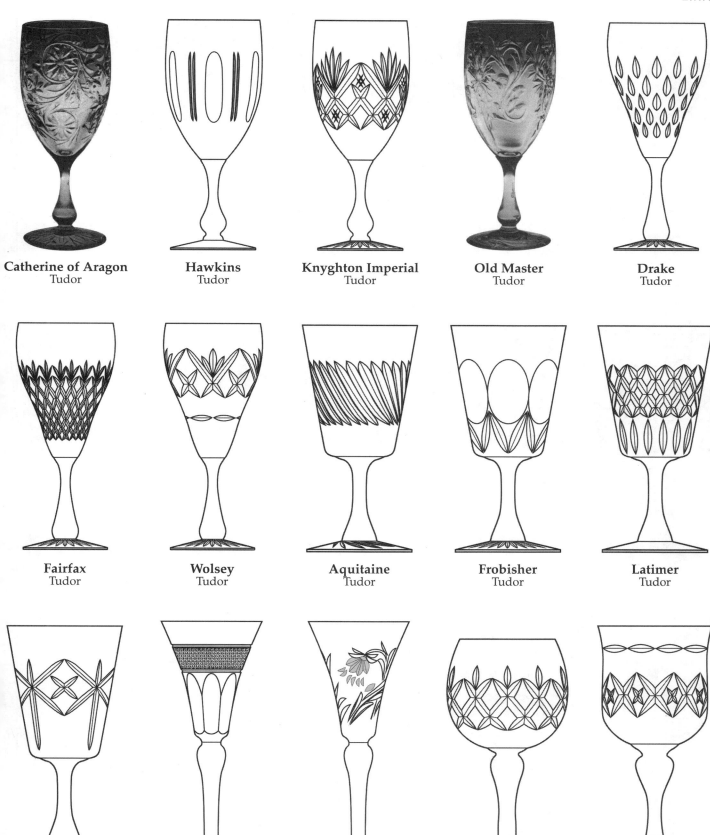

Catherine of Aragon
Tudor

Hawkins
Tudor

Knyghton Imperial
Tudor

Old Master
Tudor

Drake
Tudor

Fairfax
Tudor

Wolsey
Tudor

Aquitaine
Tudor

Frobisher
Tudor

Latimer
Tudor

Walsingham
Tudor

Castile
Tudor

Isabella
Tudor

Beaufort
Tudor

Brandon
Tudor

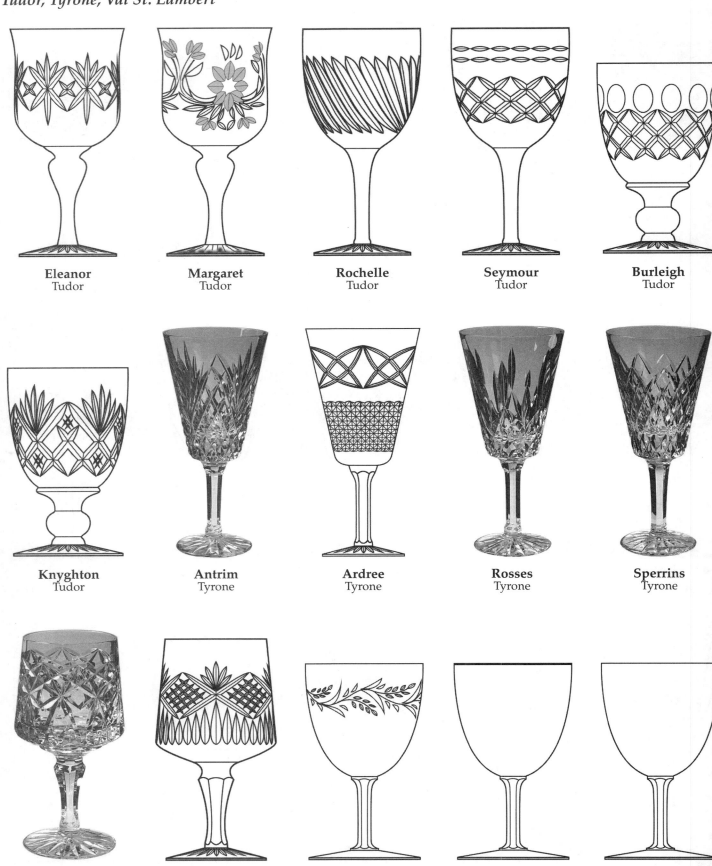

Eleanor
Tudor

Margaret
Tudor

Rochelle
Tudor

Seymour
Tudor

Burleigh
Tudor

Knyghton
Tudor

Antrim
Tyrone

Ardree
Tyrone

Rosses
Tyrone

Sperrins
Tyrone

Doonaree
Tyrone

Slieve Donard
Tyrone

Ferndale
Val St. Lambert

Glamour
Val St. Lambert
Gold Trim

Louise
Val St. Lambert

Caprice
Val St. Lambert

Gavotte
Val St. Lambert

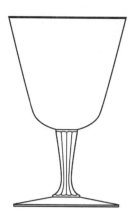

Prelude
Val St. Lambert
Platinum Trim, 8 Sides

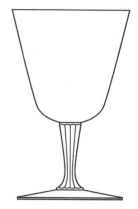

Symphony
Val St. Lambert

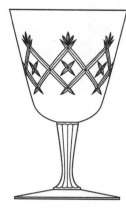

VAS 2
Val St. Lambert

Melody
Val St. Lambert

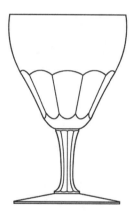

Riviera
Val St. Lambert

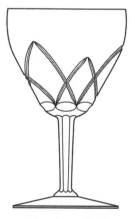

Montana Cut
Val St. Lambert

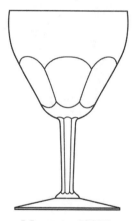

Montana TCPL
Val St. Lambert

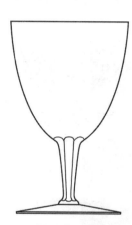

Kussnacht
Val St. Lambert

Tyrol
Val St. Lambert

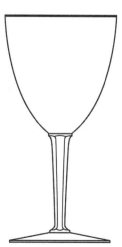

Prelude
Val St. Lambert
Platinum Trim, 5 Sides

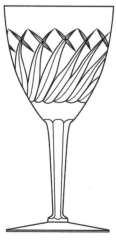

Gevaert 3/1943
Val St. Lambert

Gevaert Arlene
Val St. Lambert

Gevaert Carlton
Val St. Lambert

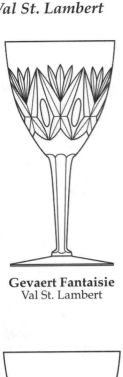

Gevaert Fantaisie
Val St. Lambert

Gevaert TCPL
Val St. Lambert

Sonata
Val St. Lambert

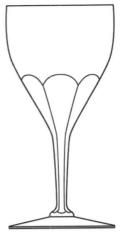

Elegance TCPL
Val St. Lambert

Nestor Hamlet
Val St. Lambert

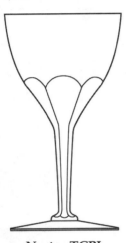

Nestor TCPL
Val St. Lambert

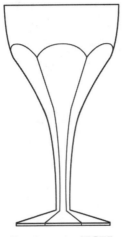

Legagneux TCPL
Val St. Lambert

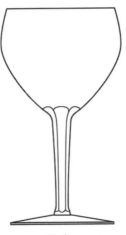

Delta
Val St. Lambert

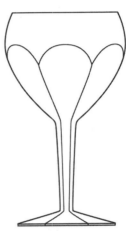

Siebel TCPL
Val St. Lambert

Osram Fantaisie
Val St. Lambert

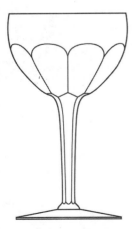

Osram TCPL
Val St. Lambert

Zermatt 6/1943
Val St. Lambert

Zermatt Avon
Val St. Lambert

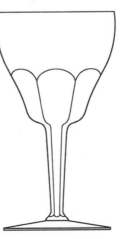

Zermatt TCPL
Val St. Lambert

Seraing 4/1948
Val St. Lambert

Seraing 5/1943
Val St. Lambert

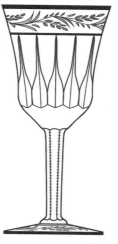

Cambrai D'Or
Val St. Lambert

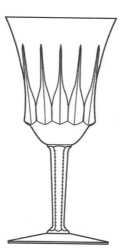

Poitiers
Val St. Lambert

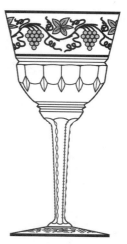

Pampre D'Or
Val St. Lambert
Gold Inlay

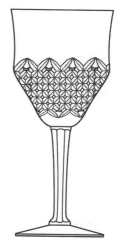

Normandy
Val St. Lambert

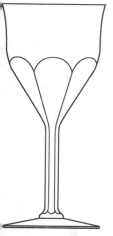

ince Evéque Torsade
Val St. Lambert

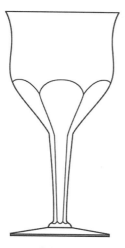

Orestes
Val St. Lambert

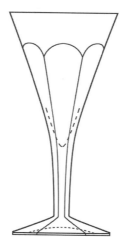

Hafnia
Val St. Lambert

VAS 1
Val St. Lambert
Gold Trim and Design

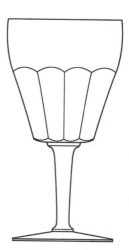

Mery TCPL
Val St. Lambert

Colonial TCPL
Val St. Lambert

Fidelio
Val St. Lambert

Goethe Millet
Val St. Lambert

Goethe TCPL
Val St. Lambert
aka "Amalfi"

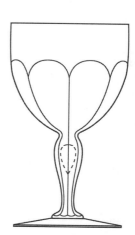

Paul I TCPL
Val St. Lambert

Val St. Lambert

Calvados Cavendish
Val St. Lambert

Berncastel
Val St. Lambert

Eurydice
Val St. Lambert

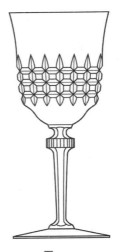

Tenor
Val St. Lambert

Balmoral
Val St. Lambert

Faradet
Val St. Lambert

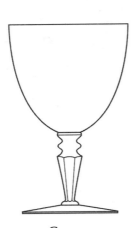

Casper
Val St. Lambert

Caro
Val St. Lambert

Concerto
Val St. Lambert

Vintage
Val St. Lambert
Gold Leaves

Walton
Val St. Lambert

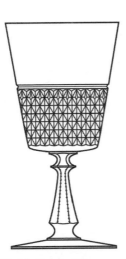

Heidelberg Diamond
Val St. Lambert

Heidelberg II
Val St. Lambert
Etched 1901

Glendale
Val St. Lambert

Granada
Val St. Lambert

Senlis
Val St. Lambert

Florian
Val St. Lambert

Crown
Val St. Lambert

Crown Gold
Val St. Lambert
Gold Trim

State Biseaux
Val St. Lambert

State Oxford
Val St. Lambert

State Plain
Val St. Lambert

State Regent
Val St. Lambert

Blarney
Val St. Lambert

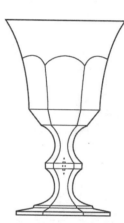

Metternich TCPL
Val St. Lambert

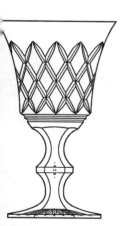

Metternich Fantaisie
Val St. Lambert

Cathedrale Napoleon
Val St. Lambert

Dans de Flor
Val St. Lambert
Gold, Cathedral Shape

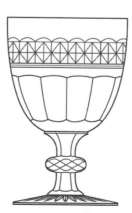

Charles X
Val St. Lambert

Kent York
Val St. Lambert

Yale 1/1953
Val St. Lambert

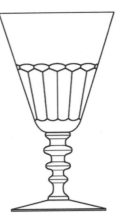

Theodule
Val St. Lambert

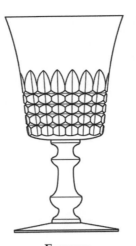

Esneux
Val St. Lambert

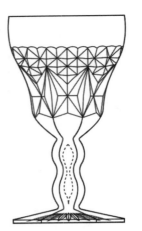

Lalaing Fantaisie
Val St. Lambert

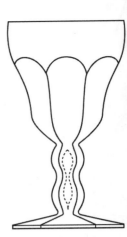

Lalaing TCPL
Val St. Lambert

Queen Anne
Val St. Lambert

St. Helene
Val St. Lambert

Gondole Losanges
Val St. Lambert

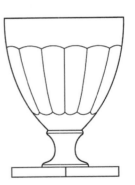

Gondole TCPL
Val St. Lambert

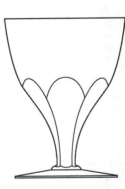

Berry TCPL
Val St. Lambert

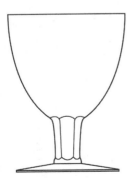

Pully
Val St. Lambert

Pully Stars
Val St. Lambert
aka "Letoile"

Allegro
Val St. Lambert

Neville
Val St. Lambert
aka "Nevel"

Major
Val St. Lambert

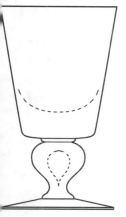

Empire
Val St. Lambert

Mirage
Val St. Lambert

Vignes
Val St. Lambert

Clarence
Val St. Lambert

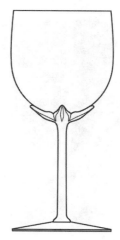

Petulia
Val St. Lambert

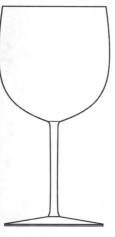

Laeken
Val St. Lambert

Laeken Decor 1903
Val St. Lambert

President
Val St. Lambert

Academie Du Vin
Val St. Lambert
Wine Tasting Series, White Wine

Brussells
Val St. Lambert
Tableware

Allison
Viking
Various Colors

Arlington
Viking
Various Colors

Ashley
Viking
Various Colors

Excelsior
Viking
Various Colors

Georgian
Viking
Various Colors

Mt. Vernon
Viking

Prelude
Viking
Long Stem

Prelude
Viking
Short Stem

VBC 2
Villeroy & Boch

Accent
Villeroy & Boch

Allegorie
Villeroy & Boch

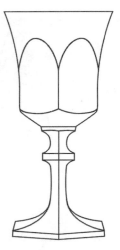

Ambassador
Villeroy & Boch

Anemone
Villeroy & Boch

Arabelle
Villeroy & Boch

Aragon
Villeroy & Boch

Avila
Villeroy & Boch

Belvedere
Villeroy & Boch

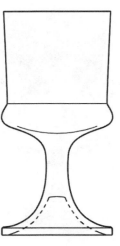

Bergamo
Villeroy & Boch

Bernadotte
Villeroy & Boch

Calypso
Villeroy & Boch

Candida
Villeroy & Boch

Charleston
Villeroy & Boch
Wine

Colonnade
Villeroy & Boch

Connaisseur
Villeroy & Boch

Contessa
Villeroy & Boch

rystal Cocktail Club
Villeroy & Boch

Désirée
Villeroy & Boch

Dover
Villeroy & Boch
High Ball

Flamenco
Villeroy & Boch
Clear and Frosted Cuts

Florina
Villeroy & Boch

Imperial
Villeroy & Boch

Iris
Villeroy & Boch

Laguna
Villeroy & Boch

Lotus Blossom
Villeroy & Boch
Gold Trim

Lugano
Villeroy & Boch

319

Malindi
Villeroy & Boch
Four Sided Stem

Malta
Villeroy & Boch

Margarita
Villeroy & Boch

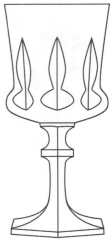

Mars 2000
Villeroy & Boch

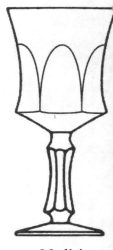

Medici
Villeroy & Boch

Metternich
Villeroy & Boch

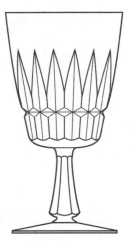

Mexicana
Villeroy & Boch

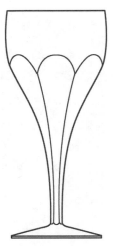

Milano
Villeroy & Boch

Monaco
Villeroy & Boch
Various Colors

Octavie
Villeroy & Boch

Orangerie
Villeroy & Boch
Wine

Paloma Picasso
Villeroy & Boch
Highball

Phoenix
Villeroy & Boch
4823

Piano
Villeroy & Boch

Roma
Villeroy & Boch

Rose
Villeroy & Boch

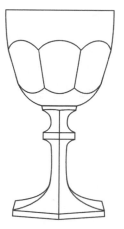

Schonbrunn
Villeroy & Boch

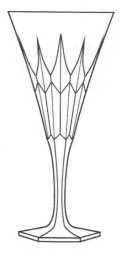

Serenade
Villeroy & Boch

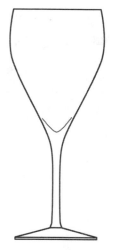

Torino
Villeroy & Boch

Treveris
Villeroy & Boch

Tulipe
Villeroy & Boch
Various Colors

VIS 1
Vistra

VIS 2
Vistra

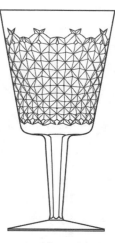

Alana
Waterford

Ashling
Waterford

Baltray
Waterford

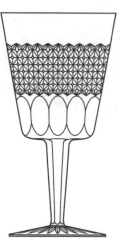

Cara
Waterford

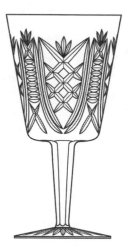

Clare
Waterford

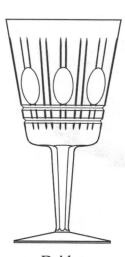

Deidre
Waterford

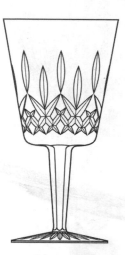

Lismore
Waterford

Waterford

Michele
Waterford

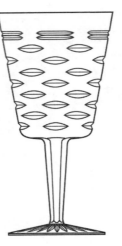

Tralee
Waterford

Araglin
Waterford

Carina
Waterford

Castlemaine
Waterford

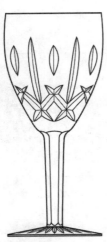

Derrymore
Waterford

Golden Araglin
Waterford
Gold Trim

Golden Carina
Waterford
Gold Trim

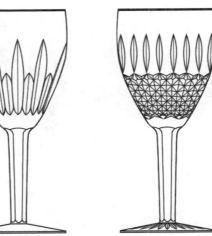

Golden Castlemaine
Waterford
Gold Trim

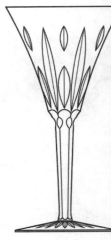

Ardree
Waterford

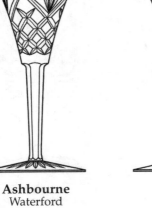

Ashbourne
Waterford

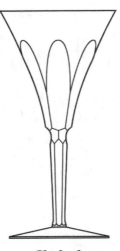

Clodagh
Waterford

Dungarvin
Waterford

Kilbarry
Waterford

Kilrush
Waterford

Avoca
Waterford

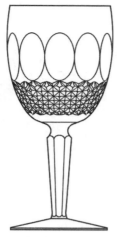

Colleen
Waterford
Tall Stem

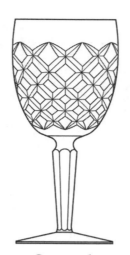

Comeragh
Waterford

Dunloe
Waterford

Glencairn
Waterford

Glengarriff
Waterford

Kildare
Waterford

Slane
Waterford

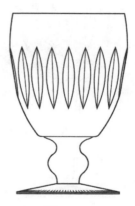

Blarney
Waterford

Boyne
Waterford

Cashel
Waterford

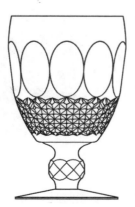

Colleen
Waterford
Short Stem

Donegal
Waterford

Kathleen
Waterford

Kilcash
Waterford

Waterford

Maureen
Waterford

Kerry
Waterford
Older, Ball Stem

Castletown
Waterford

Curraghmore
Waterford

Powerscourt
Waterford

Ballylee
Waterford

Ballymore
Waterford

Clara
Waterford

Kerry
Waterford
Newer

Kincora
Waterford

Ballyshannon
Waterford

Drogheda
Waterford

Roscrea
Waterford

Adare
Waterford

Dunmore
Waterford

Eileen
Waterford

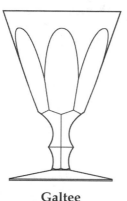

Galtee
Waterford

Mourne
Waterford

Tramore
Waterford

Glandore
Waterford

Glenmore
Waterford

Maeve
Waterford

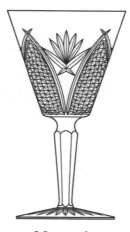

Mooncoin
Waterford

Rossmore
Waterford

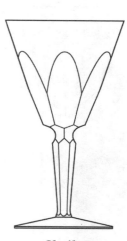

Sheila
Waterford

Templemore
Waterford

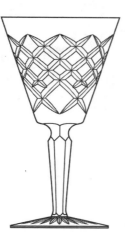

Tyrone
Waterford

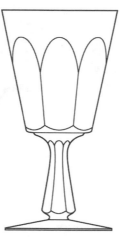

Glencree
Waterford

Kenmare
Waterford

Kinsale
Waterford

Waterford

Kylemore
Waterford

Rosslare
Waterford

Golden Lismore
Waterford
Gold Trim

Kelsey
Waterford

Leana
Waterford

Grenville
Waterford
Gold Trim

Lucerne
Waterford

Wynnewood
Waterford

Carleton
Waterford
Gold or Platinum Trim

Shandon
Waterford

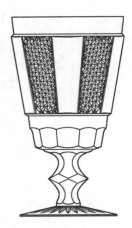

Hibernia
Waterford

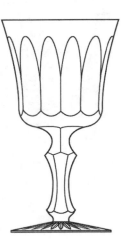

Innisfáil
Waterford

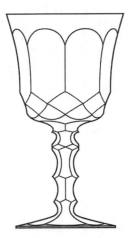

Royal Tara
Waterford

Pallas
Waterford

Laurent
Waterford "Marquis"

Merano
Waterford "Marquis"

Provence
Waterford "Marquis"

Calais
Waterford "Marquis"

Saxony
Waterford "Marquis"

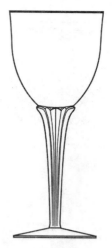

Eternity
Waterford "Marquis"
Gold Trim

Melodie
Waterford "Marquis"
Gold Trim

Destiny
Waterford "Marquis"

Avalon
Waterford "Marquis"

Chelsea
Waterford, "Marquis"
Gold Trim

Hanover
Waterford "Marquis"
Gold or Platinum Trim

Winfield
Waterford "Marquis"
Gold or Platinum Trim

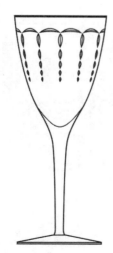

Aillion
Waterford "Marquis"
Gold Trim

Allaire
Waterford "Marquis"

Arcadia
Waterford "Marquis"

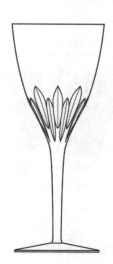

Claria
Waterford "Marquis"
Also with Gold Trim

Firenze
Waterford "Marquis"
Gold Trim

Bermuda
Waterford "Marquis"
Various Colors

Cheney
Watford

WEC 1
Webb Corbett

WEC 2
Webb Corbett

WEC 3
Webb Corbett

WEC 4
Webb Corbett

Allison
Webb Corbett

Angelique
Webb Corbett

Canterbury
Webb Corbett

Clifton
Webb Corbett

Georgian
Webb Corbett

Julia
Webb Corbett

Kensington
Webb Corbett

Leonore
Webb Corbett

Marquis
Webb Corbett

Pirouette
Webb Corbett

Prince Charles
Webb Corbett

Royal
Webb Corbett

Sherwood
Webb Corbett
Wafer Stem

Sherwood
Webb Corbett
6 Sided Stem

Warwick
Webb Corbett
6 Sided Stem

Warwick
Webb Corbett
Ball Stem

York
Webb Corbett

Conifer
Thomas Webb
53038

Dennis Diamonds
Thomas Webb
52194, Wine

Heirloom
Thomas Webb
32030, aka "Balmoral"

London
Thomas Webb
53192

Normandy
Thomas Webb
9433

Regency
Thomas Webb
53272

Thomas Webb, Wedgwood

Royal Yacht
Thomas Webb

Russell
Thomas Webb

St. Andrews
Thomas Webb
32040

Warwick
Thomas Webb
53343

Wellington
Thomas Webb
B170

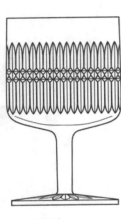

Blakeney
Wedgwood

Calendore
Wedgwood

Cheslyn
Wedgwood

Circa
Wedgwood

Coronet
Wedgwood

Crown
Wedgwood
Various Colors

Dynasty
Wedgwood

Flamenco
Wedgwood

Imperial
Wedgwood

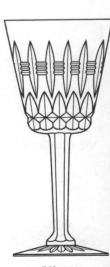

Kings
Wedgwood

Majesty
Wedgwood

Monarch
Wedgwood

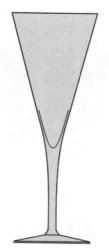

Olivia
Wedgwood
Light Smoke

Porto
Wedgwood

Royal Gold
Wedgwood

Royal Platinum
Wedgwood

Sandra
Wedgwood

Sovereign
Wedgwood

Theo
Wedgwood
Smoke

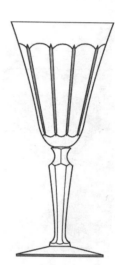

Tiara
Wedgwood

Bamboo
West Virginia Glass
843

Iridescent Lustre
West Virginia Glass
3840, Loop Optic

Princess Platinum
West Virginia Glass
1960

Rose Lustre
West Virginia Glass
40

Royal
West Virginia Glass
1960, Bright Gold Trim

1776
Westmoreland Glass
Various Colors, aka "Colonial"

American Hobnail
Westmoreland Glass
77, Various Colors

Ashburton
Westmoreland Glass
1855, Various Colors

Della Robbia
Westmoreland Glass
Clear, Milk Glass, or Ruby Flashed

English Hobnail
Westmoreland Glass
Round Base

English Hobnail
Westmoreland Glass
Square Base

Harvest
Westmoreland Glass
Amber Flashed

Old Quilt
Westmoreland Glass
500, Milk Glass

Paneled Grape
Westmoreland Glass
1881, Various Colors

Princess Feather
Westmoreland Glass

Thousand Eye
Westmoreland Glass

Waterford
Westmoreland Glass
1932, aka "Wakefield"

Herbstlaub
Wittwer
Wine

Mozell
Wittwer

Sabrina
Wittwer

Venezia
Wittwer

WDC 1
Woodmere Studio
Black

Floral Jewels
Woodmere Studio

Cherry
L. G. Wright

Moon & Stars
L. G. Wright

Sweetheart
L. G. Wright

Wild Rose
L. G. Wright

Miscellaneous Plain: These patterns do not have a cutting or an etching for a decoration. They may have gold or platinum bands.

UNK 114
Gray Bowl

UNK 305
Gray Bowl

UNK 269
Gold Trim

UNK 247
Black

UNK 268
Platinum Bands

UNK 243

UNK 179
Blue Bowl

UNK 262
Platinum Bands

UNK 259
Gold Bands

UNK 238

UNK 289
Light Blue

UNK 198
Light Blue Bowl

UNK 180
Gray

Miscellaneous Etched Patterns

UNK 234

UNK 103

UNK 117
Gold Encrusted

UNK 278
Yellow

UNK 314

UNK 106
Gold Encrusted

UNK 130
Gold Encrusted

UNK 115
Blue Bowl

UNK 244
Blue Bowl

UNK 288

UNK 132

UNK 246

UNK 101

Miscellaneous Cut Patterns

UNK 204

UNK 107

UNK 208

UNK 257

UNK 167

UNK 225

UNK 326

UNK 169
Blue Base

UNK 215

UNK 277

UNK 273
Platinum Trim

UNK 320

UNK 156
Blue Base

UNK 118

UNK 274

UNK 196

UNK 328

UNK 315

UNK 163
Black Base

UNK 150

UNK 116

UNK 239

UNK 295

UNK 187

UNK 122

UNK 306

UNK 219

UNK 154

Festival
Unknown

UNK 172

UNK 276

UNK 242

UNK 111

UNK 318

UNK 256

UNK 301

UNK 165

UNK 182

UNK 146

UNK 110

UNK 147	**UNK 201**	**UNK 211**	**UNK 212**	**UNK 108**
UNK 105	**UNK 152**	**UNK 267**	**UNK 135**	**UNK 258**
UNK 121	**UNK 197**	**UNK 213** Red Base	**UNK 321**	**UNK 142**

UNK 158	UNK 112	UNK 253	UNK 175	UNK 224
UNK 162	UNK 260	UNK 294	UNK 299	UNK 333
UNK 334	UNK 329	UNK 220	UNK 149	UNK 134

UNK 185   **UNK 129**   **UNK 120**   **UNK 307**   **UNK 316**

UNK 296   **UNK 236**   **UNK 177**   **UNK 202**   **UNK 298**

UNK 125   **UNK 317**   **UNK 217**   **UNK 252**   **UNK 240**

UNK 218   **UNK 327**   **UNK 302**   **UNK 250**   **UNK 113**

UNK 319   **UNK 330**   **UNK 153**   **UNK 235**   **UNK 231**

UNK 287   **UNK 141**   **UNK 203**   **UNK 192**   **UNK 104**

| UNK 229 | UNK 285 | UNK 331 | UNK 232 | UNK 171 |

| UNK 283 | UNK 137 | UNK 265 | UNK 272 | UNK 332 |

| UNK 207 | UNK 174 | UNK 223 | UNK 178 | UNK 161 |

UNK 109 UNK 189 UNK 143 UNK 102

UNK 313 UNK 136 UNK 157 UNK 164

UNK 166 UNK 144 UNK 249 UNK 200 UNK

Miscellaneous Pressed Patterns

UNK 311

UNK 241

UNK 216

Pattern Index

354

356

Pattern	Manufacturer	Page
Rothschild	Noritake	228
Rowena	Bryce	25
Roxane	Lalique	176
Roxbury	Cambridge	42
Roxy	Heisey	146
Roxy	Josair	167
Royal	Doyen	63
Royal	Edinburgh	73
Royal	Fostoria	82
Royal	Lalique	176
Royal	Moser	221
Royal	Webb Corbett	329
Royal	West Virginia Glass	331
Royal Baroness	Reynolds	246
Royal Crown	Mikasa	215
Royal Devon	Gorham	130
Royal Diamond	Fine Arts	74
Royal Gold	Wedgwood	331
Royal Highlights	Princess House	241
Royal Irish	Galway	120
Royal Jamestown	Mikasa	194
Royal Lace (2)	Duncan	67
Royal Manor	Mikasa	213
Royal Orchid	Noritake	224
Royal Peacock	Justin Tharaud	300
Royal Pierpont	Noritake	224
Royal Platinum	Society	281
Royal Platinum	Wedgwood	331
Royal Splendor	Society	281
Royal Tara	Waterford	326
Royal Tivoli	Gorham	129
Royal Vienna	Gorham	129
Royal Yacht	Thomas Webb	330
Royale	Lenox	184
Royale	Sasaki	271
Royale	Schott-Zwiesel	276
Royalty	Royal Leerdam	265
RPC 1	Royal Prestige	267
Rubato	Royal Leerdam	264
Rubiat	Gorham	126
Ruby	Duncan	64
Ruby	Ebeling & Reuss	71
Ruby Crown	Colony	49
Rummer	Dartington	61
Russell	Thomas Webb	330
Rut	Kosta/Boda	169
Rutledge	Fostoria	100

✿ S ✿

Pattern	Manufacturer	Page
Sabrina	Wittwer	332
Sacavem	Atlantis	7
Safir	Kosta/Boda	170, 173
Saga	Hadeland	136
Sahara	Orrefors	235
Sails	Hoya	154
Saint Hubert	Lalique	176
Salem	Susquehanna	298
Salina	Susquehanna	298
Salisbury	Stuart	295
Salon	Fostoria	98
Salutation	Noritake	224
Samara	Rosenthal	257
Samba	Kosta/Boda	175
Sampler	Fostoria	98
San Francisco	Fostoria	116
San Marino	Sasaki	271
Sandlewood	Hoya	155
Sandra	Reizart	243
Sandra	Wedgwood	331
Sandwich	Duncan	63
Sanibel	American Stemware	3
Sanssouci	Rosenthal	254
Santa Mesa	Oneida	230
Santarem	Atlantis	7
Saphir taille Lance	Cristal d'Arques	52
Sapphire	Lenox	180
Sara	Atlantis	7
Sara	Colony	49
Saranac	Morgantown	218
Saratoga	Duncan	64
Saratoga	Lenox	181
Saratoga	Rogaska	250

Pattern	Manufacturer	Page
Saratoga	Rosenthal	254
SAS 1	Sasaki	268
SAS 2	Sasaki	268
SAS 3	Sasaki	268
SAS 4	Sasaki	268
SAS 5	Sasaki	268
Satin Ribbons	Fostoria	116
Saturn	Colony	49
Saturn	Heisey	141
Saturn	Mikasa	207
Saturn	Oneida	231
Saumur	Cristal d'Arques	53
Sauvignon	Mikasa	202
Savannah	Cristal de Sevres	57
Savannah	Fostoria	111
Savoy	Mikasa	196
Savoy	Stuart	291
Saxony	Waterford	327
Saybrooke	Fostoria	99
Scanada	Holmegaard	154
Sceptre	Fostoria	95
Schleirglass	Rosenthal	257
Schonbrunn	Villeroy & Boch	321
Scroll	Dansk	60
Scroll	Imperial Glass	161
Sculptura II	Smith Glass	280
SCZ 2	Schott-Zwiesel	275
SCZ 3	Schott-Zwiesel	273
SCZ 4	Schott-Zwiesel	274
Sea Glade	Heisey	147
Sea Horse	Bayel	18
Sea Horse	Heisey	150
Sea Mist	Mikasa	211
Sea Mist	Orrefors	231
Sea Swirl	Lenox	185
Seascape	Fostoria	117
Seasons	Javit	163
Selection	Schott-Zwiesel	278
Selma	Fostoria	98
Senator	Iittala	157
Senator	Stuart	295
Senlis	Val St. Lambert	315
Senorita	Schott-Zwiesel	274
Sentiment	Lenox	180
Sentimental	Fostoria	108
September Song	Mikasa	199, 206
Sequoia	Lenox	181
Seraing 4/1948	Val St. Lambert	312
Seraing 5/1943	Val St. Lambert	313
Serena	Gorham	133
Serenade	Edinburgh	73
Serenade	Fostoria	106
Serenade	Spode	285
Serenade	Towle	307
Serenade	Villeroy & Boch	321
Serene	Lenox	182
Serene	Royal Moselle	267
Serenity	Fostoria	114
Sereno	Spiegelau	283
Sergio	Sasaki	271
Setubal	Atlantis	7
Seventeen	Tiffin	304
Sevigne	Baccarat	12
Seville	Fostoria	82
Seville	Mikasa	199
Seville	Sasaki	272
Sextette	Morgantown	220
Seymour	Tudor	310
Shadow	Mikasa	195
Shadow Rose	Rosenthal	252
Shaftesbury	Stuart	296
Shandon	Waterford	326
Shannon	Cavan	45
Shannon	Galway	119
Shannon	Royal Crystal Rock	261
Shannon	Tipperary	305
Sharon	Bryce	26
Sharon	Dartington	61
Sheelin	Cavan	45
Sheffield	Duncan	64
Sheffield	Fostoria	108
Sheffield	Gorham	128
Sheffield	Heisey	145

Pattern	Manufacturer	Page
Sheila	Waterford	325
Shelburne	Cambridge	42
Shell & Tassel	Duncan	63
Shell Pearl	Fostoria	102
Shenandoah	Lenox	181
Sheraton	Fostoria	92, 108
Sherbrooke	Royal Doulton	261
Sheridan	Rogaska	248
Sherman	Fostoria	82
Sherwood	Duncan	65
Sherwood	Fostoria	84
Sherwood	Webb Corbett	329
Shirley	Fostoria	96
Shirley	Spode	285
Shooting Stars	Fostoria	93
Short Tulip	Baccarat	10
Sicily	Cambridge	38
Siebel TCPL	Val St. Lambert	312
Sierra	Toscany	306
Signature	Cristal d'Arques	51
Sigrid	Swedish	299
Silhouette	Edinburgh	73
Silhouette	Fostoria	109
Silhouette	Lenox	188
Silhouette	Reizart	244
Silhouette	Towle	307
Silhouette (2)	Josair	167
Silk	Sasaki	272
Silk Flowers	Mikasa	194
Silver Band	Dorothy Thorpe	63
Silver Chalice	Ransgil	241
Silver Dawn	Susquehanna	298
Silver Flutes	Fostoria	100
Silver Jubilee	Schott-Zwiesel	274
Silver Lace	Import Associates	162
Silver Mist	Fostoria	87
Silver Mist	Lenox	179
Silver Mist	Mikasa	199
Silver Shadow	Lenox	184
Silver Surf	Mikasa	206
Silver Thistle	Franconia	118
Silver Twist	Reizart	245
Silver Wheat	Cambridge	33
Silver Wheat	Susquehanna	298
Silves	Atlantis	7
Silvia	Orrefors	234
Simone	Bohemia	20
Simone	Moncrief	216
Simplicity	Bryce	21
Simplicity	Cambridge	43
Simplicity	Dansk	60
Simplicity	Duncan	69
Simplicity	Fostoria	96
Simplicity	Imperial Glass	158
Simplicity	Mikasa	206
Simplicity	Noritake	226
Simplicity	Susquehanna	298
Simplicity (2)	Royal Leerdam	266
SIN 1	Sinclair	280
Singapore	Heisey	147
Sintra	Atlantis	8
Six Point Star (2)	Susquehanna	297
Skal	Rosenthal	258
Skanda	Imperial Glass	160
Skol	Denby	62
Sky Blossoms	Lenox	180, 189
Skye	Edinburgh	73
Skyflower	Fostoria	103
Skylark	Fostoria	103
Skyline	Heisey	151
Skyline	Mikasa	211
Slane	Waterford	323
Slieve Donard	Tyrone	310
Slievenamon	Tipperary	305
Small Cloverleaf	Fostoria	82
Snow Blossom	Gorham	132
Snowflower	Bryce	23
Snowflower	Rosenthal	257
Society	Fostoria	94
Soho	Rogaska	250
Soiree	Rosenthal	257
Solar	Oneida	231
Solenn II Engraved	Kosta/Boda	173

Pattern	Manufacturer	Page	Pattern	Manufacturer	Page	Pattern	Manufacturer	Page
Sunrise Medallion	Morgantown	217	Tea Rose	Mikasa	194	TOY 1	Toscany	305
Sunrise Medallion (2)	Morgantown	218	Teakwood	Hoya	155	Tracery	Lenox	183
Sunset	Gorham	131	Teardrop	Corcoran	50	Tradition	Ceska	47
Sunup	Imperial Glass	159	Teardrop	Duncan	67	Tradition	Imperial Glass	160
Superior	Lenox	188	Temple Blossom	Lenox	180	Tradition	Spiegelau	282
Surprise	Pasco	238	Templemore	Waterford	325	Traditional	Bryce	27
SUS 1	Susquehanna	297	Tempo	Bryce	29	Tralee	Waterford	322
SUS 2	Susquehanna	298	Tempo	Cambridge	40	Tramore	Waterford	325
SUS 3	Susquehanna	298	Tempo	Duncan	68	Tranquility	Fine Arts	74
SUS 4	Susquehanna	296	Tempo	Fostoria	99	Transition	Block	19
Susan	Orrefors	232	Tempo	Gorham	126	Transition	Fostoria	86
Sussex	Heisey	140	Tempo	Heisey	151	Traube	Nachtmann	223
Sutherland	Edinburgh	73	Tenderly	Lenox	183	Trefoil	Heisey	142
Sutton	Toscany	306	Tenderly	Mikasa	195	Trellis	Fostoria	99
Sutton Place	Lenox	180	Tenderness	Fostoria	113	Trellis	Heisey	141
Sutton Place	Mikasa	207	Tenor	Val St. Lambert	314	Trend	Thomas	301
Sutton Point	Mikasa	198	Terese	Galway	120	Treveris	Villeroy & Boch	321
Suzanna	Ceska	47	Terrace	Duncan	67, 70	Treves	Lalique	177
Svelte	Imperial Glass	161	Terrace	Mikasa	214	Trevi	St. Louis	288
Sven	Orrefors	234, 237	Texas	Baccarat	14	Trevi	Treasure House	308
Swanlake	Rogaska	250	Texas	Kosta/Boda	174	TRH 1	Treasure House	308
Sweet Ad-O-Line	Heisey	141	The Pines	Cambridge	33	Trianon	Bayel	18
Sweet Briar	Heisey	145	The Ritz	Mikasa	212	Trianon	Duncan	66
Sweet Home	Noritake	226	Thea	Duncan	68	Trianon	Mikasa	208, 216
Sweet Melody	Mikasa	205	Theme Gold	Gorham	128	Trianon	St. Louis	288
Sweet Swirl	Noritake	229	Theo	Wedgwood	331	Trilon	Rogaska	249
Sweetheart	Cambridge	43	Theodule	Val St. Lambert	316	Trinity	Gorham	127
Sweetheart	L. G. Wright	333	Theresa	Peill	240	Triomphe	Christian Dior	47
Sweetheart Rose	Fostoria	107	Theresia	Josair	167	Triomphe	Gorham	126
Sweetheart Rose	Johann Haviland	164	Thistle	Fostoria	102	Triomphe	Mikasa	214
Sweetheart Rose	Reizart	244	Thistle	St. Louis	288	Tripole	Duncan	65
Swirl	Dansk	60	Thistle (2)	Edinburgh	73	Tristan	Duncan	65
Swirl	Fostoria	104	Thousand Eye	Westmoreland	332	Triumph	Cambridge	38, 43
Swirl	Morgantown	221	Three Faces	Duncan	63	Triumph	Fostoria	112
Swirl	Reizart	241	Thumbprint	Morgantown	221	Triumph	Mikasa	216
Swirlette	Blefeld & Co.	18	Thunderbird	Fostoria	109	Trojan	Fostoria	90
Swizzle	Sasaki	272	Tiara	Ceska	47	Trojan (3)	Heisey	143
Sydney	Bohemia	20	Tiara	Duncan	66	Tropicana	Rosenthal	252
Sylvan	Fostoria	102	Tiara	Fostoria	100, 111	Trousseau	Fostoria	105
Sylvia	Heisey	147	Tiara	Mikasa	202	Trousseau	Imperial Glass	159
Sylvia	Nachtmann	223	Tiara	Reizart	244	Trousseau	Mikasa	199
Symmetry	Mikasa	203	Tiara	Royal Leerdam	265	Troy	Noritake	224
Symphone	Heisey	148	Tiara	Spiegelau	283	True Love	Fostoria	105
Symphony	Bryce	25	Tiara	Susquehanna	297	Trumpet	Cambridge	44
Symphony	Cambridge	39	Tiara	Towle	308	Tucano	Sasaki	272
Symphony	Ceska	47	Tiara	Wedgwood	331	Tudor	Schott-Zwiesel	274
Symphony	Edinburgh	73	TIF 1	Tiffin	301	Tudor	Towle	307
Symphony	Fostoria	103	TIF 2	Tiffin	301	Tudor Gold	Towle	307
Symphony	Josair	167	TIF 3	Tiffin	301	Tuileries	Lalique	177
Symphony	Mikasa	195, 208	TIF 4	Tiffin	301	Tuilleries/Villandry	Cristal d'Arques	55
Symphony	Orrefors	234	TIF 5	Tiffin	301	Tulip	American Cut	2
Symphony	Spode	285	TIF 6	Tiffin	301	Tulip	Fostoria	96
Symphony	Stuart	296	Tiffany	Nachtmann	223	Tulip	Mikasa	212
Symphony	Toscany	306	Tiffany	Schott-Zwiesel	275	Tulip	Rosenthal	255
Symphony	Val St. Lambert	311	Tiger Lily	Mikasa	203	Tulip	Schmid	273
			Tiger Lily	Royal Brierley	259	Tulip (2)	Bryce	20, 27
T			Tintern	Atlantis	8	Tulip Aquarius	Bryce	25
			Tintern	Stuart	292	Tulip Rays	Rosenthal	256
Tacite	St. Louis	288	Titania	Heisey	143, 145, 146	Tulipa	Block	19
Tahoe	Noritake	223	Titien	Cristal de Sevres	57	Tulipe	Sasaki	272
Talia	Mikasa	212	Tivoli	Dansk	60	Tulipe	Villeroy & Boch	321
Talisman Rose	Cambridge	44	Tivoli	Gorham	129	Tulipe D'Or	Oscar de la Renta	238
Tally Ho	Cambridge	33	Tivoli	Rosenthal	258	Tulipwood	Hoya	155
Tally Ho	Heisey	152	Tivoli	Thomas	301	Tundra	Svend Jensen	164
Tamara	Spiegelau	282	Tivoli Copenhagen	Holmegaard	154	Turin	Baccarat	14
Tangen	Hadeland	136	TMC 1	Thomas	300	Turkey Eagle	Bryce	30
Tangent	Kosta/Boda	173	Toccata	Peill	240	Turkey Eagle	Lenox	190
Tango	Rogaska	251	Today	Cambridge	32	Turning Point	Noritake	227
Tango	Royal Leerdam	266	Today	Imperial Glass	159	Tuscany	Rogaska	250
Tango	Schott-Zwiesel	276	Tommy	St. Louis	288	Tuxedo	Lenox	180
Tanja	Josair	167	Topas	Nachtmann	223	Tuxedo	Mikasa	208, 215
Tapestries	Dansk	60	Topaz Lustre	Dorothy Thorpe	63	Tuxedo	Reizart	242
Tapestry	Fostoria	87	Torino	Villeroy & Boch	321	Tuxedo Gold	Oscar de la Renta	238
Tapio	Iittala	157	Tornade	Cristal d'Arques	56	Tweed	Edinburgh	73
Tara	Fostoria	114	Tosca	Lalique	177	Twilight	Fostoria	107
Tara Gold	Rogaska	249	Tosca	Oneida	229	Twilight	Gorham	125
Tarantella	Schott-Zwiesel	276	Tosca	Spiegelau	281	Twilight	Lenox	186
Tarn	St. Louis	288	Toselli	Mikasa	204	Twilight	Lenox	189
Tartan	Lenox	190	Toselli	Spiegelau	282	Twilight Blossoms	Lenox	189
Tastevin	Baccarat	9	Touch of Spring	Mikasa	201	Twilight Shadow	Lenox	184
Tatting	Heisey	141	Toujours	Oneida	230	Twin Oaks	Mikasa	196
Tavastia	Iittala	157	Touraine	Duncan	67	Twinkle	Toscany	306
Taylor	Kosta/Boda	172	Tourville	Baccarat	15	Twist	Heisey	140
						Twist	Imperial Glass	158
						Twist	Spiegelau	283

Pattern	Manufacturer	Page
Tyrol	Sussmuth	299
Tyrol	Val St. Lambert	311
Tyrolean	Heisey	149
Tyrone	Waterford	325

❧ U ❧

Pattern	Manufacturer	Page
Ulla	Josair	167
Ulrica	Kosta/Boda	168
Ultima Thule	Iittala	157
Ultra	Rosenthal	256
Undine	Spiegelau	281
Unity	Lenox	186
Uptown	Mikasa	201
Ursula	Dansk	60
Uzes Satine	Cristal d'Arques	52

❧ V ❧

Pattern	Manufacturer	Page
Vail	Fostoria	85
Val d'Oise	Baccarat	13
Val De Loire	Baccarat	13
Valencay	Cristal d'Arques	54
Valencia	Cambridge	33, 37, 39
Valencia	Gorham	124
Valencia	Imperial Glass	158
Valencia	Stuart	295
Valerie	Crystal Clear Ind.	57
Valley Lily	Imperial Glass	158
Valmy	Lorraine	193
Van Dijck	Royal Leerdam	265
Van Wyck	Bryce	24
Vanborough	Royal Doulton	262
Vanderbilt	Mikasa	197
Variation (2)	Rosenthal	254
VAS 1	Val St. Lambert	313
VAS 2	Val St. Lambert	311
Vasa	Orrefors	237
VBC 2	Villeroy & Boch	318
Vega	American Cut	2
Vega	Baccarat	11
Vendome	Noritake	227
Vendome taille Lance	Cristal d'Arques	56
Vendome Uni	Cristal d'Arques	56
Venetian	Mikasa	205
Venetian Gold	Mikasa	205
Venetian Opal	Mikasa	206
Venetian Star	Easterling	71
Venezia	Wittwer	333
Venice	Mikasa	205
Veninga	Central Glass	46
Venise	Fostoria	113
Venitienne	Cartier	45
Ventoux	Cristal d'Arques	55
Venture	Fostoria	113
Venture	Lenox	185
Venus	Astral	4
Venus	Bayel	18
Venus	Fostoria	110
Venus	Heisey	147
Venus	Holmegaard	154
Venus	Spiegelau	283
Vermeil	Fostoria	110
Vernon	Fostoria	82
Verona	Fostoria	83
Veronique	Sasaki	272
Versailles	Cristal d'Arques	53
Versailles	Fostoria	90, 113
Versailles	Josair	167
Versailles	Mikasa	199
Versailles	Morgantown	219
Versailles	Sasaki	272
Versailles	Stuart	291
Verve	Schott-Zwiesel	275
Vesper	Fostoria	89, 106
Vesta	Spiegelau	282
Via Veneto	Spiegelau	283
Viceroy	Lenox	188
Vicomte	Cristal d'Arques	51
Victoria	Fostoria	104
Victoria	Import Associates	162
Victoria	Orrefors	233
Victoria	Rosenthal	253

Pattern	Manufacturer	Page
Victoria	Royal Leerdam	264
Victoria	Stuart	292
Victoria	Stuart	293
Victoria Regina	Morgantown	220
Victorian	Fostoria	87
Victorian	Heisey	141
Victory	Cambridge	43
Victory	Duncan	67
Victory	Fostoria	80
Victory	Heisey	142
Victory Wreath	Cambridge	39
Vie en Rose	Gorham	133
Vienna	Edinburgh	73
Vienna	Peill	240
Vienne	Baccarat	11
Viewpoint	Noritake	228
Vignes	Val St. Lambert	317
Ville de Lyon	Fabergé	74
Villeneuve	Cristal d'Arques	55
Vincennes	Baccarat	11
Vincent	Kosta/Boda	170
Vine	Bryce	23
Vine	Reizart	242
Vineyard	Lenox	188
Vintage	Cambridge	35
Vintage	Fostoria	81, 85
Vintage	Orrefors	233
Vintage	Val St. Lambert	314
Vintage Grape	Imperial Glass	160
Virginia	Fostoria	80, 86
Virginia	Morgantown	219
Virginia	St. Louis	288
Virginia Dare	Duncan	64
Virginian	Cambridge	39
Virna	Toscany	306
Virtue	Noritake	224
VIS 1	Vistra	321
VIS 2	Vistra	321
Viscount	Gorham	124, 128
Viscount	Josair	167
Viscount	Mikasa	209
Vision	Mikasa	212
Vision	Morgantown	220
Vision	Orrefors	233
Vista	Mikasa	208
Vista	Noritake	227
Viva	Kosta/Boda	173
Viva	Kosta/Boda	175
Viva	Schott-Zwiesel	278
Viva Satin	Schott-Zwiesel	278
Vogue	Fostoria	108
Vogue	Josair	167
Vogue	Mikasa	211
Vogue	Rogaska	249
Vogue	Schott-Zwiesel	279
Volnay	Baccarat	9
Volnay	Lalique	177
Voltaire	Baccarat	10
Volterra	Schott-Zwiesel	275

❧ W ❧

Pattern	Manufacturer	Page
Wabash	Heisey	142
Waikiki	Heisey	146
Wakefield	Bryce	29
Wakefield	Fostoria	97
Wakefield - see Waterford	Westmoreland	332
Waldorf	Oscar de la Renta	238
Wales	Bryce	26
Wales Laurel	Bryce	27
Walsingham	Tudor	309
Walton	Val St. Lambert	314
Warwick	Royal Brierley	258
Warwick	Thomas Webb	330
Warwick (2)	Webb Corbett	329
Washington	Cristal d'Arques	52
Washington	Denby	62
Washington	Fostoria	80
Waterbury	Fostoria	90
Watercolors	Block	19
Watercress	Fostoria	94
Waterford	Duncan	63
Waterford	Westmoreland	332

Pattern	Manufacturer	Page
Watteau	Cristal de Sevres	57
Wavecrest	Fostoria	94
Wavemere	Fostoria	99
Waverly	Heisey	149
WDC 1	Woodmere Studio	332
Weatherly	Lenox	184
WEC 1	Webb Corbett	328
WEC 2	Webb Corbett	328
WEC 3	Webb Corbett	328
WEC 4	Webb Corbett	328
Wedding Band	Cambridge	35, 38, 40
Wedding Band	Celebrity	45
Wedding Band	Heisey	151
Wedding Band	Oscar de la Renta	238
Wedding Day	American Manor	2
Wedding Flower	Fostoria	110
Wedding Promises	Lenox	189
Wedding Ring	Fostoria	101
Wedding Ring	Johann Haviland	164
Wedding Rings	Cambridge	44
Wedding Rose	Cambridge	38
Wedge Cut	Rosenthal	254
Wellesley	Royal Doulton	263
Wellington	Fostoria	92
Wellington	Holmegaard	154
Wellington	Thomas Webb	330
Wessex	Schott-Zwiesel	275
Wessex Gold	Schott-Zwiesel	275
Westbury	Stuart	291
Westchester	Fostoria	93
Westchester	Heisey	149
Westerleigh	Noritake	227
Westerly	Towle	308
Westminster	Fostoria	92, 106
Westminster	Gorham	132
Westminster	Libbey/Rock Sharpe	193
Westminster	Mikasa	200
Westminster	Royal Brierley	259
Westminster	Royal Doulton	262
Westminster	Schott-Zwiesel	275
Weston Court	Stuart	291
Westport	American Stemware	3
Westwood	Pasco	239
Wheat	Fostoria	101
Wheat	Heisey	139
Wheat	Kosta/Boda	171
Wheat	Lenox	179
Wheat	Reizart	241, 244
Wheat	Rosenthal	253
Wheat	Sasaki	272
Wheat	Toscany	307
Wheaton	Mikasa	197
Whirlpool	Heisey	141
Whisper	Fostoria	107
White Echo	Lenox	179
White House	Bryce	28
Whitehall	Colony	50
Wickham	Hawkes	136
Wild Rose	Duncan	70
Wild Rose	Imperial Glass	158
Wild Rose	L. G. Wright	333
Wildflower	Cambridge	36, 41
Wildflower	Fine Arts	74
Wildflower	Lenox	179
Will o' the Wisp	Heisey	146
Williamsburg	Bryce	29
Williamsburg	Fostoria	105
Willow	Astral	4
Willow	Duncan	70
Willow	Fostoria	97
Willowmere	Fostoria	97
Wilma	Fostoria	94
Wilmington	Bryce	26
Wilshire	Mikasa	216
Wimbledon	Fostoria	114
Wimbledon	Mikasa	196
Winchester	Royal Brierley	259
Winchester	Stuart	293
Wind Drift	Mikasa	207
Wind Swept	Mikasa	195
Windermere	Stuart	290
Windfall	Fostoria	102
Windham	Towle	308

Pattern	Manufacturer	Page
Windows	Sasaki	272
Windsor	Fostoria	101
Windsor	Imperial Crystals	157
Windsor	Mikasa	200
Windsor	Royal Brierley	259
Windsor	Royal Doulton	261
Windsor	Stuart	295
Windsor Park	Mikasa	208
Windswept	Lenox	186
Windswept	Noritake	225
Winfield	Gorham	132
Winfield	Waterford	327
Wings	Sasaki	272
Winsor	Cambridge	42
Winter Berry	Imperial Glass	159
Wintersong Gold	Oneida	230
Winthrop	Pasco	239
Wistar	Fostoria	84
Wistaria	Duncan	68
Wisteria	Mikasa	201
Wolsey	Tudor	309
Wonderful	Pasco	239
Wood Violet	Susquehanna	297
Wood Violet	Susquehanna	299
Woodchester	Stuart	294
Wooddale	Stonegate	290
Woodflower	Bryce	25
Woodland	Fostoria	80, 86
Worcester	Imperial Crystals	157
Wreath	Bryce	23
Wreath	Susquehanna	297
Wyndcrest	Reizart	245
Wynnewood	Waterford	326

❧ Y ❧

Pattern	Manufacturer	Page
Yale	Toscany	307
Yale 1/1953	Val St. Lambert	316
Ye Olde Ivy	Cambridge	35
Yeoman	Heisey	140
York	Fostoria	86, 91
York	Royal Brierley	260
York	Stuart	292
York	Towle	308
York	Webb Corbett	329
York I	Kosta/Boda	168
Young Love (2)	Javit	163

❧ Z ❧

Pattern	Manufacturer	Page
Zephyr	Atlantis	8
Zermatt 6/1943	Val St. Lambert	312
Zermatt Avon	Val St. Lambert	312
Zermatt TCPL	Val St. Lambert	312
Zest	Gorham	135
Zeuse	Heisey	147
Zodiac	Imperial Glass	160
Zurich	Baccarat	13

❧ #'s ❧

Pattern	Manufacturer	Page
1" Club	Gorham	126
1	Peill	239
1	Stuart	290
3	Stuart	290
4	Stuart	290
4-1	Bryce	26
4	Hawkes	136
2	Hawkes	136
-1	Hawkes	136
-1	Stuart	290
-1	Glastonbury/Lotus	121
-1	Stuart	291
-660	Bohemia	19
-1	Duncan	65
-1	Stuart	292
-1	Glastonbury/Lotus	121
-2	Glastonbury/Lotus	121
-3	Glastonbury/Lotus	121
-1	Stuart	293
-1	Glastonbury/Lotus	121
-2	Glastonbury/Lotus	121

Pattern	Manufacturer	Page
56-1	Susquehanna	296
67-1	Glastonbury/Lotus	121
67-2	Glastonbury/Lotus	121
67-3	Glastonbury/Lotus	122
75-1	Glastonbury/Lotus	122
77-3	Glastonbury/Lotus	122
78-1	Glastonbury/Lotus	122
78-2	Glastonbury/Lotus	122
80-1	Glastonbury/Lotus	122
80-2	Glastonbury/Lotus	122
81-1	Glastonbury/Lotus	122
85-1	Glastonbury/Lotus	122
89-1	Glastonbury/Lotus	122
94-1	Glastonbury/Lotus	122
97-2	Glastonbury/Lotus	122
98-2	Glastonbury/Lotus	122
235-1	Bryce	23
331-1	Seneca	279
388-5	Seneca	279
430-1	Rosenthal	253
450-1	Rosenthal	253
460-1	Rosenthal	253
470-1	Glastonbury/Lotus	122
484-5	Seneca	279
485-3	Seneca	279
503-1	Duncan	67
515-5	Seneca	279
553-1	Glastonbury/Lotus	122
553-2	Glastonbury/Lotus	123
575-1	Bryce	29
625-1	Bryce	29
638-1	Bryce	28
638-2	Bryce	28
688-1	Bryce	29
688-2	Bryce	29
740-1	Bryce	28
740-2	Bryce	28
740-3	Bryce	28
761-1	Bryce	28
766-1	Fostoria	80
771-1	Bryce	22
784-1	Bryce	24
784-2	Bryce	24
784-3	Bryce	24
784-4	Bryce	24
784-5	Bryce	24
785-1	Bryce	23
798-1	Bryce	25
854-1	Bryce	28
854-2	Bryce	28
854-3	Bryce	28
865-1	Bryce	24
865-2	Bryce	24
866-1	Bryce	25
866-2	Bryce	25
866-3	Bryce	25
879-1	Bryce	29
886-1	Bryce	27
895-1	Bryce	26
896-1	Bryce	26
896-1	Glastonbury/Lotus	123
913-3	Seneca	279
913-4	Seneca	279
934-1	Bryce	26
942-1	Bryce	24
942-2	Bryce	24
943-1	Bryce	22
945-1	Bryce	26
965-2	Glastonbury/Lotus	123
969-1	Glastonbury/Lotus	123
984-1	Glastonbury/Lotus	123
997-1	Reizart	243
1001-3	Libbey/Rock Sharpe	191
1004-3	Libbey/Rock Sharpe	191
1004-4	Libbey/Rock Sharpe	191
1007-5	Libbey/Rock Sharpe	191
1013-4	Libbey/Rock Sharpe	191
1023-2	Libbey/Rock Sharpe	191
1023-3	Libbey/Rock Sharpe	191
1041-1	Bryce	20
1066	Cambridge	32
1235-1	Seneca	279
1258 ½-2	Seneca	279

Pattern	Manufacturer	Page
1500-1	Glastonbury/Lotus	123
1500-2	Glastonbury/Lotus	123
1776	Westmoreland	332
2000-2	Rosenthal	252
2000-3	Rosenthal	252
2000-3	Tiffin	301
2003-2	Libbey/Rock Sharpe	191
2006-4	Libbey/Rock Sharpe	191
2008-1	Glastonbury/Lotus	123
2008-4	Libbey/Rock Sharpe	191
2008-5	Libbey/Rock Sharpe	191
2009-10	Libbey/Rock Sharpe	191
2010-8	Libbey/Rock Sharpe	191
2010-9	Libbey/Rock Sharpe	191
2011-16	Libbey/Rock Sharpe	192
2011-17	Libbey/Rock Sharpe	192
2011-18	Libbey/Rock Sharpe	192
2011-19	Libbey/Rock Sharpe	192
2014-3	Libbey/Rock Sharpe	192
2201-3	Hawkes	136
3000-1	Rosenthal	254
3001-4	Libbey/Rock Sharpe	192
3003-6	Libbey/Rock Sharpe	192
3003-7	Libbey/Rock Sharpe	192
3004-1	Libbey/Rock Sharpe	192
3004-2	Libbey/Rock Sharpe	192
3005-18	Libbey/Rock Sharpe	192
3005-19	Libbey/Rock Sharpe	192
3006-12	Libbey/Rock Sharpe	192
3006-13	Libbey/Rock Sharpe	192
3006-14	Libbey/Rock Sharpe	192
3006-15	Libbey/Rock Sharpe	193
3007-7	Libbey/Rock Sharpe	193
3007-8	Libbey/Rock Sharpe	193
3007-9	Libbey/Rock Sharpe	193
3010-1	Libbey/Rock Sharpe	193
3010-2	Libbey/Rock Sharpe	193
3101	Orrefors	237
3114-1	Cambridge	35
3120-1	Cambridge	36
3355-1	Heisey	142
3400-1	Imperial Glass	158
3400-2	Imperial Glass	158
3720-1	Glastonbury/Lotus	123
5082-1	Fostoria	88
5097-1	Fostoria	89
6003-1	Heisey	151
6016-1	Fostoria	94
6030-1	Hawkes	136
6268	Steuben	288
7586-1	Morgantown	219
7630-1	Morgantown	218
7643-1	Morgantown	217
7643-2	Morgantown	217
7643-3	Morgantown	217
7643-4	Morgantown	217
7666	Steuben	288
7685-1	Morgantown	219
7691-1	Morgantown	218
7691-2	Morgantown	218
7725	Steuben	289
7737	Steuben	289
7846	Steuben	289
7877	Steuben	289
7917	Steuben	289
7924	Steuben	289
7925	Steuben	289
7926	Steuben	289
8011	Steuben	289
15003-1	Tiffin	302
15022-1	Tiffin	302
15024-1	Tiffin	302
15032-1	Tiffin	302
15042-3	Tiffin	302
15065-1	Tiffin	302
15067-2	Tiffin	302
15067-3	Tiffin	302
15070-2	Tiffin	302
15071-1	Tiffin	302
15072-3	Tiffin	302
15073-3	Tiffin	302
15073-4	Tiffin	303
15074-5	Tiffin	303

Pattern	Manufacturer	Page
15074-6	Tiffin	303
15082-3	Tiffin	303
15083-1	Tiffin	303
15088-2	Tiffin	303
17323-1	Tiffin	303
17323-2	Tiffin	303
17348-5	Tiffin	303
17361-2	Tiffin	303
17371-1	Tiffin	303
17492-2	Tiffin	303
17505-1	Tiffin	304
17551-3	Tiffin	304
17566-3	Tiffin	304
17594-13	Tiffin	304
17596-2	Tiffin	304
17623-5	Tiffin	304
17664-2	Tiffin	305

❧ Unknowns ❧

Pattern	Manufacturer	Page
UNK 101	Unknown	336
UNK 102	Unknown	345
UNK 103	Unknown	335
UNK 104	Unknown	343
UNK 105	Unknown	340
UNK 106	Unknown	336
UNK 107	Unknown	337
UNK 108	Unknown	340
UNK 109	Unknown	345
UNK 110	Unknown	339
UNK 111	Unknown	339
UNK 112	Unknown	341
UNK 113	Unknown	343
UNK 114	Unknown	334
UNK 115	Unknown	336
UNK 116	Unknown	338
UNK 117	Unknown	335
UNK 118	Unknown	338
UNK 120	Unknown	342
UNK 121	Unknown	340
UNK 122	Unknown	338
UNK 125	Unknown	342
UNK 129	Unknown	342
UNK 130	Unknown	336
UNK 132	Unknown	336
UNK 134	Unknown	341
UNK 135	Unknown	340
UNK 136	Unknown	345
UNK 137	Unknown	344
UNK 141	Unknown	343
UNK 142	Unknown	340
UNK 143	Unknown	345
UNK 144	Unknown	345
UNK 146	Unknown	339
UNK 147	Unknown	340
UNK 149	Unknown	341
UNK 150	Unknown	338
UNK 152	Unknown	340

Pattern	Manufacturer	Page
UNK 153	Unknown	343
UNK 154	Unknown	339
UNK 156	Unknown	338
UNK 157	Unknown	345
UNK 158	Unknown	341
UNK 161	Unknown	345
UNK 162	Unknown	341
UNK 163	Unknown	338
UNK 164	Unknown	345
UNK 165	Unknown	339
UNK 166	Unknown	345
UNK 167	Unknown	337
UNK 169	Unknown	337
UNK 171	Unknown	344
UNK 172	Unknown	339
UNK 174	Unknown	344
UNK 175	Unknown	341
UNK 177	Unknown	342
UNK 178	Unknown	344
UNK 179	Unknown	334
UNK 180	Unknown	335
UNK 182	Unknown	339
UNK 185	Unknown	342
UNK 187	Unknown	338
UNK 189	Unknown	345
UNK 192	Unknown	343
UNK 196	Unknown	338
UNK 197	Unknown	340
UNK 198	Unknown	335
UNK 200	Unknown	345
UNK 201	Unknown	340
UNK 202	Unknown	342
UNK 203	Unknown	343
UNK 204	Unknown	337
UNK 207	Unknown	344
UNK 208	Unknown	337
UNK 211	Unknown	340
UNK 212	Unknown	340
UNK 213	Unknown	340
UNK 215	Unknown	337
UNK 216	Unknown	346
UNK 217	Unknown	342
UNK 218	Unknown	343
UNK 219	Unknown	339
UNK 220	Unknown	341
UNK 221	Unknown	345
UNK 223	Unknown	344
UNK 224	Unknown	341
UNK 225	Unknown	337
UNK 229	Unknown	344
UNK 230	Unknown	338
UNK 231	Unknown	343
UNK 232	Unknown	344
UNK 234	Unknown	335
UNK 235	Unknown	343
UNK 236	Unknown	342
UNK 238	Unknown	334
UNK 239	Unknown	338
UNK 240	Unknown	342
UNK 241	Unknown	346

Pattern	Manufacturer	Page
UNK 242	Unknown	33_
UNK 243	Unknown	33_
UNK 244	Unknown	33_
UNK 246	Unknown	33_
UNK 247	Unknown	33_
UNK 249	Unknown	34_
UNK 250	Unknown	34_
UNK 252	Unknown	34_
UNK 253	Unknown	34_
UNK 256	Unknown	33_
UNK 257	Unknown	33_
UNK 258	Unknown	34_
UNK 259	Unknown	33_
UNK 260	Unknown	34_
UNK 262	Unknown	33_
UNK 265	Unknown	34_
UNK 267	Unknown	34_
UNK 268	Unknown	33_
UNK 269	Unknown	33_
UNK 272	Unknown	34_
UNK 273	Unknown	33_
UNK 274	Unknown	33_
UNK 276	Unknown	33_
UNK 277	Unknown	33_
UNK 278	Unknown	33_
UNK 283	Unknown	34_
UNK 285	Unknown	34_
UNK 287	Unknown	34_
UNK 288	Unknown	33_
UNK 289	Unknown	33_
UNK 294	Unknown	34_
UNK 295	Unknown	33_
UNK 296	Unknown	34_
UNK 298	Unknown	34_
UNK 299	Unknown	33_
UNK 301	Unknown	33_
UNK 302	Unknown	34_
UNK 305	Unknown	33_
UNK 306	Unknown	33_
UNK 307	Unknown	34_
UNK 311	Unknown	34_
UNK 313	Unknown	34_
UNK 314	Unknown	33_
UNK 315	Unknown	33_
UNK 316	Unknown	34_
UNK 317	Unknown	34_
UNK 318	Unknown	33_
UNK 319	Unknown	34_
UNK 320	Unknown	33_
UNK 321	Unknown	34_
UNK 326	Unknown	33_
UNK 327	Unknown	34_
UNK 328	Unknown	3_
UNK 329	Unknown	34_
UNK 330	Unknown	34_
UNK 331	Unknown	34_
UNK 332	Unknown	34_
UNK 333	Unknown	34_
UNK 334	Unknown	34_

Manufacturer Index

Manufacturer Index (continued)

Listed below are many of the manufacturers pictured in this guide that mark or *sign* their glassware. Some of the makers will almost always mark their glassware, while others will only mark certain patterns or lines. Names with a "•" will *sign* most of their product — some unmarked product in that company could signify a second quality piece. In parentheses are some of ways the manufacturer will *sign* a product other than by using their own name.

Astral
Atlantis
Baccarat•
Bayel
Cartier•
Ceska
Christian Dior•
Cristal de Sevres
Dartington
Daum•
Edinburgh•
Fabergé•
Fostoria
Galway
Gorham
Hawkes•
Josair (crown symbol)
Kosta/Boda (Kosta or Boda)
Lalique•
Ralph Lauren•
Lenox• (Lenox or Script L in wreath; a second
        is indicated with a broken circle in the
        logo)
Libbey
Lorraine•
Moser•
Noritake

Oneida (intertwined OC)
Orrefors• (of)
Peill• (P)
Riedel
Rogaska
Rosenthal• (script R)
Royal Brierley• (Royal Brierley or Brierley)
Royal Doulton• (Royal Doulton or a crown)
Schott-Zweisel (Z in a block)
Seneca
Sinclair
Spiegelau (S)
Spode•
St. Louis•
Steuben•
Stuart•
Theriesenthal
Tiffin
Tipperary•
Tudor•
Tyrone•
Val St. Lambert• (Val St Lambert or VSL)
Villeroy/Boch
Waterford•
Webb Corbett• (Webb Corbett or a crown)
Thomas Webb• (Thomas Webb or Webb)
Wedgwood

Replacements, Ltd.

The World's Largest Retailer of Discontinued and Active China, Crystal, Flatware, and Collectibles

In 1981, Bob Page, an accountant turned flea marketer, founded Replacements, Ltd. Since then, the company's growth and success can only be described as phenomenal.

Today, Replacements, Ltd. locates hard-to-find pieces in over 70,000 patterns — some of which have not been produced for more than 100 years. Now serving over 1.8 million customers, with an inventory of 3.5 million pieces, they mail up to 250,000 inventory listings weekly to customers seeking additional pieces in their patterns.

The concept for Replacements, Ltd. originated in the late 1970s when Page, then an auditor for the state of North Carolina, started spending his weekends combing flea markets buying china and crystal. Before long, he was filling requests from customers to find pieces they could not locate.

"I was buying and selling pieces primarily as a diversion," Page explains. "Back when I was an auditor, no one was ever happy to see me. And, quite frankly, I wasn't thrilled about being there either."

Page began placing small ads in shelter publications and started building a file of potential customers. Soon, his inventory outgrew his attic, where he had been storing the pieces, and it was time to make a change. "I'd be up until one or two o'clock in the morning. Finally, I took the big step: I quit my auditing job and hired one part-time assistant. Today, I'm having so much fun, I often have to remind myself what day of the week it is!"

Replacements, Ltd. continued to grow quickly. In fact, in 1986, *Inc. Magazine* ranked Replacements, Ltd. 81st on its list of fastest-growing independently-owned companies in the U.S. "Our growth has been incredible," says Page, who was named 1991 North Carolina Entrepreneur of the Year. "I had no idea of the potential when I started out."

Clear standards of high quality merchandise and the highest possible levels of customer service are the cornerstones of the business, resulting in a shopping experience unparalleled in today's market place. Page also attributes much of the success of Replacements, Ltd. to a network of nearly 1,500 dedicated suppliers from all around the U.S. The company currently employs about 500 people in an expanded 225,000 square foot facility (the size of four football fields).

Another major contributor to the company's fast growth and top-level customer service is the extensive computer system used to keep track of the inventory. This state of the art system also maintains customer files, including requests for specific pieces in their patterns. It is maintained by a full-time staff of over 20 people and is constantly upgraded to ensure customers receive the information they desire quickly and accurately.

For those who are unsure of the name and/or manufacturer

Greensboro, North Carolina, Facility

Some of the 50,000 shelves in the 225,000 square foot warehouse

of their patterns, Replacements, Ltd. also offers a free pattern identification service. In addition, numerous books and publications focusing on pattern identification have been published by Replacements, Ltd. for both suppliers and individuals.

Replacements, Ltd. receives countless phone calls and letters from its many satisfied customers. Some need to replace broken or lost items while others want to supplement the sets they have had for years. A constant in the varied subjects customers write about is their long and fruitless search — a search that ended when they learned what Replacements, Ltd. could offer. "Since many patterns are family heirlooms that have been handed down from generation to generation, most customers are sentimental about replacing broken or missing pieces," Page says. "It's a great feeling to help our customers replace pieces in their patterns and to be able to see their satisfaction. Like our logo says — *we replace the irreplaceable.*"

Another growing area that Replacements, Ltd. has developed for its customers is the collectibles market. The company now offers a wide range of collectibles from companies such as Bing and Grondahl, Royal Copenhagen,

Boehm, Hummel, Lladro, and many more. "It was a natural progression of our business," says Page, "and something our customers had been requesting."

The Replacements, Ltd. showroom and museum in Greensboro, NC is a 12,000 square-foot retail facility located in front of the massive warehouse. It is decorated with turn of the century hand-carved showcases, 20-foot ceilings, and classic chandeliers. Inside, one can view an incredibly varied selection of merchandise — from figurines, mugs, and ornaments to the china, crystal, and flatware that made the company famous.

The fascinating Replacements, Ltd. museum, adjacent to the retail showroom, is the home for over 2,000 rare and unusual pieces that Page has collected over the years. It includes a special section dedicated to one of Page's first loves — early twentieth century glass from companies like Tiffin, Fostoria, Heisey, Imperial, and Cambridge.

FOR MORE INFORMATION

- Call 1-800-REPLACE (1-800-737-5223 from 8 am to 10 pm Eastern Time, 7 days a week)

- Write to:
  1089 Knox Road
  PO Box 26029
  Greensboro, NC 27420

- Fax: 910-697-3100

- Visit the Replacements, Ltd. showroom and museum, at exit 132 off I-85/40 in Greensboro, NC. The showroom and museum are open 7 days a week, from 8 am to 9 pm.

A view of Replacements' 12,000 square foot showroom.

REPLACEMENTS, LTD.
"We Replace The Irreplaceable."®

1-800-REPLACE (1-800-737-5223)

B ob Page was born April 19, 1945, and grew up working the fields of his family's small tobacco farm in Ruffin, North Carolina. He attended the University of North Carolina at Chapel Hill and graduated with a degree in business and a major in accounting. After two years in the U.S. Army, he obtained his CPA certificate and worked in public accounting for eight years. In 1978, he took a position as an auditor for the state of North Carolina.

In 1981, Bob left his accounting career to start Replacements, Ltd. so he could pursue his hobby and true love — going to antique shops, flea markets, etc., locating discontinued china, crystal, and flatware patterns. In a little over 15 years, Replacements has become the world's largest retailer of discontinued and active tableware, with sales in excess of $60 million and employing 500 people. Bob has won numerous awards including Small Businessman of the Year in North Carolina, North Carolina Entrepreneur of the Year, and the Torch Award given by the Human Rights Campaign for his efforts in promoting equal rights.

D ale Frederiksen was born June 15, 1962, in Pontiac, Michigan, and attended Waterford Township High School. In 1980, Frederiksen moved to Chattanooga, Tennessee, to attend Tennessee Temple University, graduating in 1984 with a BS degree in secondary education. He taught junior and senior high mathematics in Kansas City, Kansas, before returning to Chattanooga in 1987 to teach mathematics and to coach volleyball at Ooltewah Middle School. In 1989, he joined the staff of Replacements, Ltd. as an inventory purchasing agent and later trained in the field of computer graphics, where he has created or supervised the creation of most of the images in this book. Frederiksen enjoys researching and discovering patterns that have previously been undocumented. He also enjoys accompanying his companion, Bob Page, on buying trips throughout the states and playing

with their miniature dachshunds Toby Lee and Trudy Mae. His hobbies include tennis, volleyball, and visiting flea markets.

O ther stemware identification books by Page and Frederiksen include *Tiffin is Forever*, *Seneca Glass Company*, and *A Collection of American Stemware - Glastonbury/Lotus, Libbey/Rock Sharpe, and Hawkes,* and may be purchased through Replacements, Ltd. by calling 1-800-737-5223 (1-800-REPLACE).